LIBRARY TRAINING GUIDES

Series Editor: David Baker
Editorial Assistant: Joan Welsby

Other Library Training Guides available

Training needs analysis
Michael Williamson
1-85604-077-1

Induction
Julie Parry
1-85604-078-X

Evaluation
Steve Phillips
1-85604-079-8

Training and development for women
Beryl Morris
1-85604-080-1

Interpersonal skills
Philippa Levy
1-85604-081-X

Management of training and staff development
June Whetherly
1-85604-104-2

Mentoring
Biddy Fisher
1-85604-105-0

Recruitment
Julie Parry
1-85604-106-9

Supporting adult learners
Tony Bamber *et al.*
1-85604-125-5

Presenting information
Clare Nankivell and Michael Shoolbred
1-85604-138-7

Personal professional development and the solo librarian
Sue Lacey Bryant
1-85604-141-7

Team management
Robert Bluck
1-85604-167-0

Training library assistants
Margaret Lobban
1-85604-139-5

Introduction by the Series Editor

This new series of Library Training Guides (LTGs for short) aims to fill the gap left by the demise of the old Training Guidelines published in the 1980s in the wake of The Library Association's work on staff training. The LTGs develop the original concept of concisely written summaries of the best principles and practice in specific areas of training by experts in the field which give library and information workers a good-quality guide to best practice. Like the original guidelines, the LTGs also include appropriate examples from a variety of library systems as well as further reading and useful contacts.

Though each guide stands in its own right, LTGs form a coherent whole. Acquisition of all LTGs as they are published will result in a comprehensive manual of training and staff development in library and information work.

The guides are aimed at practising librarians and library training officers. They are intended to be comprehensive without being over-detailed; they should give both the novice and the experienced librarian/training officer an overview of what should/could be done in a given situation and in relation to a particular skill/group of library staff/type of library.

David Baker

LIBRARY TRAINING GUIDES

Training for IT

Richard Biddiscombe

Library Association Publishing

Library Association Publishing is wholly owned by The Library Association.

Published by
Library Association Publishing
7 Ridgmount Street
London WC1E 7AE

First published 1997

British Library Cataloguing in Publication Data
A catalogue record for this book is available from the British Library.

ISBN 1-85604-186-7

Typeset in 11/12pt Palermo from author's disk by Library Association Publishing.
Printed and made in Great Britain by Commercial Colour Press, London.

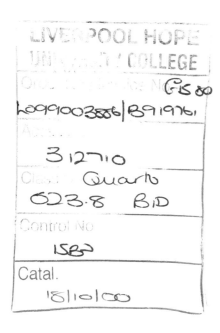

Contents

Acknowledgments

Grateful thanks are due to:

The University of Bristol, and in particular Michael Wall, for permission to reproduce the Training Needs Analysis Questionnaire (Appendix 1).

The University of Middlesex, and in particular to Maggie Steel and Jennie Wyatt of the Staff Development Unit for permission to reproduce Section 7 of the Staff Development and Training Handbook, 1996/97 (Appendix 2).

The University of Edinburgh Library, and in particular Morag Watson, the Head of Networked Information Systems, for permission to reproduce the Computing Skills Questionnaire and Computing Skills Minimum Requirements documents (Appendix 3).

Sue Rex of the University of Birmingham Staff Development Unit for her help and advice during the compilation of this publication.

Introduction

There is no doubt that the need for IT training is growing in all sectors of the economy. IT is changing the way many jobs are being performed, but it also poses questions about why some jobs need to be done at all. A re-assessment and re-evaluation of workplace activities and the workplace itself is being forced upon us. Such changes, and the challenges they present, are very evident in the library and information sector. Here IT is forcing changes in the way traditional services are organized and with the forecast growth of IT applications, through the Internet for example, it will force further re-assessment of individual roles and professional practice.

Managing the changes successfully is difficult and is made more problematic by the speed at which the process continues. Staff need to be well managed in this uncertain environment. They should be given an honest assessment of the future viability of their work and a fair evaluation of the retraining they will need. They want reassurance, help, and a sense of participation in the decision-making process. In such a situation IT training, perhaps previously offered only on an *ad hoc* basis, becomes an essential element in the process of confidence building in the workplace.

Because IT is changing many aspects of our lives, away from the workplace as well as within it, organizational needs can be seen as coinciding with the training needs of the individual. Such a mutual interest should, with the right management approach, provide a sound basis for staff development and the achievement of service objectives. It is through such a partnership approach that staff morale can be better maintained and the necessary re-assessment of jobs more satisfactorily achieved.

For those organizations that have already embraced a staff development culture the impact made upon the system by IT may be more easily absorbed through the extension of existing training programmes: for those organizations in which training is less well integrated, it is often more difficult to provide IT training as a continuous and underlying basis for the support of working practices; but it must be attempted.

Unlike the computerization of a particular technical process, such as a new library management system, IT brings all-pervading and continuous changes. A positive approach is therefore essential if an IT training programme is to be successful.

All training is expensive but the widespread application of IT in most aspects of the workplace can make training in this area particularly resource hungry. Nevertheless, effective training is essential if full benefit is to be gained from the initial investment. Some organizations have been less than keen to invest in the process, but IT training is forcing a change to this attitude for the following reasons:

- the need for training affects all levels of the organization, not just the newest recruit
- the successful operation of IT applications will improve the performance of the whole organization as well as the individuals within it

- IT changes the structure and levels of responsibilities within an organization
- the successful implementation of IT raises the morale of the organization.

IT itself can be used to provide some of the IT training that needs to be organized. Many companies have been using such methods for some time, but some computer-based training programs are more concerned to raise the profits of the firm than to create an educated staff. There are, however, a number of ways in which IT applications can be used to make IT training more efficient and better directed.

IT training and staff development

All training is an essential part of staff development. Successful organizations have staff development as a central element in their personnel policies. As Barbara Dewey states:[1]

> Training programs should be an essential part of an overall program of library development and continuing education for librarians at all levels. Library school curriculum and day-to-day work experience are no longer enough to keep librarians current with new developments in the field or satisfy the needs of their institution or their personal career growth. Staff development and comprehensive continuing education programs sponsored or at least sanctioned by institutions are essential elements of general human resources and career development policies in libraries . . . Occupational obsolescence is a critical reality in any field but is particularly so for librarians who are dealing with information and methods of accessing it that are accelerating at an enormous rate. At the same time, library clientele are becoming more sophisticated in their demands for information and expect librarians to respond to their needs in an efficient and up-to-date manner.

If the speed of change was evident when Barbara Dewey wrote this in the late eighties, it is even more so today and the need for a comprehensive staff development policy is all the more important. In the intervening years the IT element of any staff development programme has increased to such an extent that IT is now essential to almost all aspects of library and information work, indeed to the whole work process.

The challenge to the profession is undoubtedly real and many are already wringing their hands in despair. But Elspeth Hyams, speaking in 1996, is more optimistic. One of the challenges, she says, is 'not from the downsizing as a result of the industrial revolution and the shake out of white collar jobs which has a been a feature of the last decade. It is instead from the potential failure to recognize and grasp new opportunities that are already apparent to those who like to spot trends.'[2]

A survey on staff development for the IMPEL 1 project and reported by Graham Walton, project co-leader at the New tricks? conference at Bournemouth University in August 1996, found that the library staff wanted the following from a training programme:

- A basic level of computer literacy
- A long-term IT skills training programme

- A structured formalized programme
- Joint training with computer staff
- A programme geared to individual needs
- Exchange of experience with outside personnel
- Time management training.

Aims of this publication

Although the changes IT is bringing are relevant to all organizations, this book is primarily concerned with IT training in a library and information environment. This publication will be of most help to those library organizations which have not yet undertaken a coordinated approach to IT training.

In writing this publication I have come to the conclusion that, though many libraries have organized some IT training for their staff, few have developed a full scale policy, or put a full IT training programme in place. It is for this reason that there are less examples of good practice at the end of this book than I would have wished. More examples would certainly have been helpful and more instances from libraries other than academic ones would have given a more balanced view. The examples are, however, the best illustrations I could find. If this book is the consequence of inadequate research on my part, I look forward to finding out who has been leading the way in this area.

The examples I have included are intended to provide enough ideas, for staff or IT programmes, to form a working basis for developing IT training initiatives for information professionals in all types of libraries.

Although stages of IT development vary enormously over different sectors of the economy, the problems faced are relevant to all. Indeed, it is true that some libraries most advanced in terms of IT have still not produced a coordinated approach to IT training.

In terms of general principles, this book:

- outlines the broad principles upon which to base IT training
- recommends ways in which these principles can be applied to form the basis of coordinated programmes for staff training
- gives examples of current practice
- suggests ways in which IT can itself be used to facilitate training.

In terms of general practice this book:

- covers the possible options for administering IT training
- outlines the technical requirements for offering in-house training
- suggests ways in which training can be offered at minimum cost through computer assisted learning (CAL) options
- suggests possible levels of training depending on the need and functions of the staff
- outlines the possibilities of using the IT training programme to improve staff qualifications.

The publication and the series

This publication can be seen in the context of the Library Training Guides series and will have some relationship with its sister publications.

A number of titles already published will augment this publication, including *Management of training and staff development*,[3] *Training and develop-*

ment for women,[4] and *Personal professional development and the solo librarian*.[5] These are all relevant to the process of IT training and should be consulted if readers wish to develop their reading. Within these publications a number of chapter headings are particularly relevant: *Identifying training needs, Learning, Meeting training needs, Assessing training needs* and *Who is responsible for training?* are all important general aspects which augment the coverage of this work.[3] *Self motivation, A personal plan for professional development* and *Pursuing qualifications* are also useful additional reading;[5] the chapter entitled *Designing and delivering women's training and development courses* may also prove helpful in many library IT training environments.[4]

The limits of this book

For the purposes of this book the concept of IT training will be limited to broad IT functions. These include e-mail, word-processing, Internet applications, spreadsheet packages and CD-ROM and online databases. It will not specifically cover library management system training, though undoubtedly some of the recommendations will be useful when introducing staff to such systems.

References

1 Dewey, Barbara I., *Library jobs: how to fill them, how to find them*, Phoenix, Oryx Press, 1987.
2 Hyams, Elspeth, 'Professional futures — why the prospects are so rosy', *Aslib proceedings*, **48** (9), 1996, 204—8.
3 Whetherly, June, *Management of training and staff development*, London, Library Association Publishing, 1994.
4 Morris, Beryl, *Training and development for women*, London, Library Association Publishing, 1993.
5 Lacey Bryant, Sue, *Personal professional development and the solo librarian*, London, Library Association Publishing, 1995.

1 IT training in libraries

This chapter discusses the effects IT is having on the structure of the information profession and the way in which training should reflect this. While library staff should be better trained to meet the IT challenges they are facing, there is also a need for those with computing qualifications to appreciate the basis of information skills. This is essential in converged services and is growing more important throughout the profession.

1.1 Creating a new profession?

Librarians are being touched more profoundly by the IT revolution than most other professions. The changes that are occurring have an effect not only on the way tasks are undertaken, but also on the very definition of the profession itself. The education provided by university departments of information studies and supported by the professional bodies is failing, for the most part, to keep abreast of these. Continuing professional development is therefore essential now and will continue to be so.

In essence, what is being created, albeit slowly, is a new profession of information workers with a variety of different but complementary skills all working as information facilitators and providers. Barriers still exist between the traditional disciplines, even when the individuals are brought together to combine their skills. This defensiveness and sometimes mutual incompehension may be understandable but it will need to change if existing professions are to make sense of their future and bring their commitment to the service ethic into the new era.[1]

Although Elspeth Hyams is talking about the information professional in the business area, her comments have a wider relevance:

> While, due to the lack of funding, some jobs in public libraries may be disappearing, not only new but different types of 'traditional' job in service provision will be created, but that new professions and new roles are emerging and will continue to emerge as the Information Society matures. Moreover, these new professions are open to the traditional information manager, if individuals are prepared to take responsibility for aspects of their professional development and go out and learn the additional skills that they will need, to have an enviable advantage over everyone else out there, competing for the same jobs. For while it is true that the ground beneath our feet is shifting and changing, it is also true that it is doing the same thing for everyone else. The difference is that the professional information resource manager and practitioner, the manager and exploiter of business information has a unique competitive advantage over non-specialists trying to enter the brave new information world, with its new and highly desirable jobs. Provided, that is, that the individual realizes what skills he or she is blessed with and makes the most of them.[2]

To help in this the SKIP (Skills for New Information Professionals) project based at the University of Plymouth in the UK is attempting to 'define the type, range and levels of IT skills required by LIS staff in the electronic library within an organizational context'.[3]

The dramatic effects of the changes that are taking place are most clearly seen in academic libraries. In a growing number of these, departments concerned with communication and computer technology (the academic computing service) are linking with those concerned with the provision of information in various formats (the library). The level and complexity of these links vary but that there is a synergy here is evident and compelling.

These changes, so recently initiated by developments in IT, will continue to draw together those professionals and organizations concerned with information, and its delivery in its various formats. Publishing, editing, translating, database creation, computing, graphics, teaching and learning, librarianship and information science; all are being forced into a new and closer relationship through technological change.

To keep up with these developments and learn to accept the changes and pressures they bring, staff need continuous training and development in IT skills. It is essential at this time of unsettling change to ensure that such training is not only enabling them to improve their job performance, but also providing them with supportive help as they acquire new and essential skills. So far, as has been suggested, the formal educational structure has not been able to address these changes, as may be evidenced in the closing of a number of US library schools.

This is not to say that those skills traditionally needed by librarians are not wanted any more. They are still in demand, but their application is often different. New jobs are being created in which such skills have to be adapted to the electronic age. Traditional elements of library education, such as information retrieval and the reference interview, are being adapted to help in the creation of database interfaces and the provision of machine-based guidance and help. On a more basic level the need for elementary keyboard skills in order to access information is now essential for most librarians.

The delivery of information is becoming increasingly entwined with the information itself and librarians are increasingly involved in the management of network provision. The added value which electronic interfaces offer to the raw data is also an important facet of the information age. Information professionals can help ensure that users gain easy access to the information on offer through devising helpful interfaces. They should also be concerned with the quality of the information that is offered and use their influence to help achieve improvements on behalf of their users.

1.2 The development of IT in libraries

Only 25 or so years ago libraries were at the beginning of what was then called their mechanization phase. Computers were being used in batch process mode for activities such as cataloguing. At this stage, public libraries were often in the forefront of the developments for they were able to share the large computers of their parent authorities. This was the time when new companies and cooperatives, such as OCLC in the US and BLCMP in the UK, began using the 'new technology' to computerize catalogue records. Later they were able to use the data to create automated issue systems.

As each generation of these library management systems (LMS) have been developed, staff training has been provided in the adopting library during the first few weeks of its operation. In these sessions all relevant staff are brought together to undergo supervized training. This is usually organized by using a suite of terminals in a specially equipped temporary location. This form of *ad hoc* IT training has become well established over the years.

1.3 The new IT environment

We have moved beyond this less complex era of single process development. IT requires more than just a simple approach to training, for it is not about merely meeting a single objective. The IT environment is multi-tasking, all-pervading and continually developing. Consequently any IT training should be an important part of a continuous staff development programme, but ideally an independent part of it. The effectiveness with which staff cope with IT has a bearing on the self esteem and self fulfilment of individuals and, consequently, the successful operation of an organization.

Staff at all levels and in all departments need IT training. A programme should therefore be concerned with imparting and sustaining transferable skills to the workforce. Where and how this fits into the staff development policy of an institution may need to be discussed within an organization, but libraries will need to place more emphasis on this aspect than other departments.

Once initial training has been done, regular use of IT will usually improve an individual's confidence. However, because IT is continually developing there is a need for on-going training opportunities. Such changes may result from the use of new editions of software or be necessary because of hardware changes. The workplace environment may change, for example with the introduction of new operating systems, different platforms or improved networked access.

Among the IT applications that would fall within an IT training programme are:

- keyboarding skills
- basic computer skills
- word processing
- e-mail
- networking skills
- database searching
- CD-ROM databases
- Internet searching
- scanning electronic journals
- public information systems
- voice mail
- video conferencing.

1.4 IT skills, public interfaces and service level targets

The implementation of a good training scheme for improving the IT skills of staff can have a positive affect on morale and it is well known that minor improvements in the work environment can have a beneficial effect on staff productivity. Organizations that show concern for their workforce usually gain improvements in productivity.

For a service organization such as a library and information service the level of staff morale and confidence is evident in the quality of service given to its client group. In terms of IT, good training will mean a threefold benefit to the service:

- communication between staff will be more efficiently undertaken
- front-line communication with readers will be of better quality
- the teaching role of library staff will carry more authority.

The second and third of these are of growing importance. All staff who carry out front-line service roles are increasingly being asked to help users with IT problems, including word-processing, laser printing and electronic databases.

For example, the demand for enquiry desk staff assistance with CD-ROM databases is often a major focus for helping library users. The wide variety of interfaces used for these products demands a confidence and understanding that can be adequately offered only if there is a profound knowledge of interfaces and database content. A good level of IT training in this area gives staff not only the basics for understanding the structure of certain interfaces but also, when confronted with a new problem, the confidence to try alternatives when searching for solutions.

Helping a user with a database query often develops into one-to-one tuition. Therefore training is a growing aspect of librarians' work, both formally and informally. The formal approach is especially, though by no means exclusively, evident in academic libraries. Librarians are increasingly expected to organize training courses and run group sessions to mixed ability groups of various sizes. In such situations effective training on group teaching and dynamics is needed to supplement IT training, which in itself needs to cover a wider aspect of database provision than just the simple knowledge of database content and interface.

Essential elements for library trainers include:

- presentation skills
- interpersonal skills
- basic computer skills
- knowledge and basic understanding of different computer platforms
- knowledge about e-mail registration
- an understanding of e-mail technology
- Internet search skills
- Web page creation and editing skills
- experience of appropriate CD-ROM interfaces
- experience of appropriate online database interfaces
- knowledge of personal bibliographical management packages
- knowledge of access to online publications
- course organization skills
- assessment skills
- an understanding of learning techniques.

Front-line library staff at reference desks will need to cover most of these topics too, but may not need the more teaching-orientated skills demanded of a group trainer.

If these front-end and training aspects are important for the reputation of a library and information service, then so, of course, is the reputation of supporting services. Good IT skills are also essential in acquisitions, cataloguing and special collections departments.

They are important for the fulfilment of service level agreements, for example enabling the staff to work more quickly, accurately and effectively. The use of direct database access for book and periodical ordering is growing fast, with essential information being stored and retrieved using computerized housekeeping programs. In cataloguing departments the wide use of databases points to a growing need for high level IT skills, while in the special collections area there is a growing interest in the digitization of older material.[4]

Staff employed in these more discrete service areas of the library will need knowledge of how to access and use:

- suppliers' online information
- catalogue records
- online bibliographical databases
- CD-ROM databases
- Internet services
- e-mail
- appropriate software packages
- digitization.

1.5 Training needs in converged services

The IT training needs of those working in converged services may be somewhat broader than those in more traditional staff structures. The problems are more complex because there are staff from at least two separate backgrounds needing to understand the IT skills and roles of each other.

Managing converged services should be easier if appropriate training is provided. Background information as well as basic technical knowledge needs to be offered in all the discipline areas of the merged work environment. Effective IT training programmes in such situations helps to build a sense of common purpose and mutual respect, thereby helping to unify the disparate parts of the new organization.

In such situations in particular, but not exclusively, there is a need to consider the wider implications of training. When services such as computing and librarianship come together the staff involved know little about the background and context of the others' profession. In these circumstances training should help to enlighten each group about the skills and practices of the other.

A trainee, therefore should expect the training to offer:

- valuable transferable skills
- an awareness of the technological context in which the particular operation is set
- an awareness, if appropriate, of the skills, practices and approaches of different professional groups within an organization
- a basic conceptualization of operations across the converged service
- back-up support to help in undertaking the operation in future.

Formal IT training programmes need to be created to ensure that ex-library staff are offered programmes that will broaden their technological background. Penny Garrod reports that these staff need 'training in the use of the Internet (Web authoring/HTML/Java), in advanced word processing and in desk top publishing. Managers are increasingly specifying when recruiting staff that they should be IT literate, keyboard familiar, and not be "technophobic" '.[3]

The following topics may need to be offered to staff with traditional library backgrounds:

- networking technology
- mail system administration
- client-server management
- Web database management
- Web authoring and HTML
- IT support management.

Training should also be offered to ex-computing staff in converged structures in order to provide an information skills context and the user-oriented view of librarians to IT applications.

1.6 Summary

The technological changes now taking place in libraries and many other organizations mean that all staff must be proficient in basic IT skills if they are to perform the tasks for which they are employed. The better they are trained, the better they will perform and the more successful the organization will be in fulfilling its mission.

For library and information staff, or for any organization with a service role, there is a demand by users for training. This may not be a formal demand, but helping the user by explaining how information has been obtained is, or should be, a part of the user interface of any service.

To offer an effective service in an IT environment, staff must have in-depth knowledge of, and confidence in, the technology and what it can do. IT training for staff is therefore an essential investment, providing internal efficiency gains and improved service potential.

References

1 Biddiscombe, Richard (ed.), *The end-user revolution: CD-ROM, the Internet and the changing role of the information professional*, London, Library Association Publishing, 1996, 35–42.
2 Hyams, Elspeth, 'Professional futures – why the prospects are so rosy', *Aslib proceedings*, **48** (9), 1996, 204–8.
3 Garrod, Penny, 'Skills for the new professional', *Library Association record*, **98** (1), 1996, *Library technology supplement*, 99–100.
4 Wakeling, Will, 'Meeting the demand for CD-ROM databases. Case study 1: academic libraries', in Biddiscombe, Richard (ed.), *ibid*.

2 Aims and objectives of IT training

In the previous chapter we saw a few of the reasons why IT training needs to be introduced into libraries – the changing environment and user expectations demand it. This chapter outlines the aims and objectives of IT training and sets out the goals that should be set for achieving the best results from the training being offered.

2.1 Putting IT into context

Although some staff, when first confronted with the need to learn IT skills, welcome the idea and become receptive to it, most do not. Change is usually seen as threatening and, given the choice, most people would be happy to continue to do things in the traditional way. This reluctance is true for many who are already experienced in IT. When faced with having to adapt to a new edition of a software package, or a change of operating system – from DOS to Windows, for example – many are reluctant to take the leap even though they suspect it will be a change for the better.

This is partly to do with the need to overcome a steep learning curve at the start of any new process. Usually such a curve must be overcome while the pressures of work continue and, inevitably, stress levels rise as a consequence.

Convincing staff of the need to change is essentially a part of the staff development process. IT at one time was limited to the information retrieval aspects of library work, but now it is a basic element in an increasing number of processes. IT needs to be seen as an essential and growing element in the development of the individual, both in the workplace and beyond.

It should first be discussed in a broad context, for example:

- IT in the wider environment, used as an aspect of every-day life, e.g. in banking and telephony and the growing use of the Internet etc.
- IT as a benefit to the community: improvements in communication, the growing possibilities of distance learning, health care improvements etc.
- IT as the key to new employment opportunities: IT skills improve opportunities and expectations in the job market
- IT in the context of the organization: the positive aspects of the need to change work practices, working more efficiently and improving job satisfaction
- IT as the catalyst for change in the library and the information community, releasing library staff from clerical routine and offering opportunities to use their information skills in new and exciting ways.

Approaching IT training in this expansive way can be a help in making the training programme a success. It is important to involve the participants in such a way that they see the process as a positive experience which will help in their own personal professional development (PPD).

2.2 To encourage confidence in IT

Using this contextual idea is particularly important when comprehensive IT applications are being introduced in an organization for the first time, for example when a full networked office environment is launched.

The introduction of any change is always distrusted. When IT-based, this suspicion may be well founded, for IT will change most jobs in some way and may radically reduce the need for particular tasks. For example, the role of a personal secretary will change once the manager starts dealing directly with his or her own e-mail.

Introducing change not only needs to be done with some sensitivity, it has to be done efficiently and be well thought out. Consideration has to be given to the consequences of the actions to be taken. When introducing IT it is therefore important to:

- anticipate the changes in the work environment that will result
- undertake effective planning for the changes
- identify the positive ways in which staff structure and individual responsibilities will alter, and plan for the negative factors that are bound to arise
- plan the allocation of workstations, ensuring adequate access for those who need them most and appropriate access to others
- plan effectively for budgetary allocations to improve workstation access year on year
- allow for depreciation and plan for workstation replacement and upgrading
- reassure the staff that they will be learning new, transferable skills
- introduce the changes with adequate explanations to staff as groups and as individuals
- organize a comprehensive training programme for all levels of staff
- monitor progress and allow for slow or reluctant learners
- feed the results back into the training programme.

2.3 To make staff proficient in IT skills

Whether an organization is revolutionizing its work practices by introducing an IT environment or is in the process of continuing the development of its staff, IT training is important. The intention must be to make the using of IT a positive experience for employees. An adequate investment in the training programme can help to make this a reality.

It is usually not possible to provide a full training programme in-house; some skills will not be available, while back-up and support may best be provided through external courses or conferences. Some possible structures for IT training programmes are given in Chapter 4.

In addition, training opportunities exist through using IT itself in support of a training programme (see Chapter 7). Web interfaces, CAL (computer assisted learning) packages or the built-in tutorials of established computer packages can augment the training process. Information about what is available and how it can be accessed will be essential. It will also be necessary to ensure that basic skills are in place if these support options are to be used effectively.

Basic skills training in a PC environment should provide an understanding of elementary computing skills including:

- file management
- disk management
- an explanation of DOS commands
- an introduction to basic terminology
- an introduction to Windows technology
- an introduction to basic word processing.

Courses in basic computing can be done in two hours or so, giving hands-on experience at each stage of the process. Real proficiency, however, comes only through constant practice. Ideally, therefore, a training programme should be enhanced by a programme of testing and assessment. This will help ensure that the original lessons have been learned and, from an organization point of view, that a real return on investment is being made.

2.4 To give opportunities for further development

Once confidence in the basic skills has been gained, training can move on to those specific tasks that need to be learned for the job in hand. Specific training courses can be run in these, especially if a number of candidates need to undertake it. Those specialist tasks undertaken by only one or two people could possibly benefit from using a learning package, either commercially produced or developed internally.

Opportunities for further development should be notified to staff so that individuals can develop their own skills and explore new areas. Ways in which such opportunities can be notified include:

- the provision of an electronic bulletin board of forthcoming training opportunities of relevance to the staff
- encouraging access to existing Web training packages
- centrally loading training support packages
- providing support documentation for the IT training course for those who have attended training courses
- devising in-house Web training pages for particular training needs
- creating an in-house Web server to produce workable exercises and feedback.

2.5 To give staff measurable transferable skills

Transferable skills are increasingly important in a rapidly changing world. Gaining new skills is an important asset for employees in the job market. If training is adequate staff can also improve self esteem and job satisfaction. One of the aims of any IT training programme should be to give trainees sound transferable skills.

These should be seen as not only new skills which can be used in other parts of the same workplace, but also as having a wider application. The need for such training is nowhere more evident than in converged library services. Here the changes being made to traditional staff structures often require staff to learn new skills.

Improving the marketability of staff should be seen as an opportunity rather than a threat to the employing organization. IT training should raise the level of staff morale while improving the quality of recruitment. A reputation for good staff relations and an effective training culture will not deprive an organization of new applicants.

The concept of measurable transferable skills is implied in the provision of back-up exercises as part of the training process. More formally, in the UK, it can be part of the process of awarding Scottish or National Vocational Qualifications (S/NVQs). Encouraging employees to take the opportunity of improving their vocational qualifications can be part of the IT training process.[1,2]

Though involvement in such schemes may help develop a better approach to staff development, in general the IT units outlined for the library and information profession in the national scheme are not satisfactory, reflecting, as they do, a rather dated concept of IT as relevant to only a specialized few. The present units for IT training, for example, form only a small (and inadequate) part of the present Levels 2 to 4; the clear implication is that IT is limited to non-professional staff.

2.6 To encourage continuous professional development (CPD)

One of the essential aims and objectives of any training programme should be to encourage an individual to see it as part of his or her own continuous personal development. This will ultimately be to the benefit of both the organization and the wider community.

Individuals should be encouraged to develop a personal interest in their own training needs and see competence in IT as an important part of this. A continuous process of self education will improve a person's approach to his or her work and give a greater sense of personal fulfilment. Enthusiasm may also be transferred to fellow workers and help to encourage a positive work attitude to technological change.

This sense of a personal responsibility for an employee's own development cannot be stressed too much. Individual careers can be transformed when someone is determined to take his or her personal development seriously.[3] The introduction to The Library Association's *Framework for Continuing Professional Development* states: 'Your progress is largely determined by **your** job performance, **your** decisions and **your** actions. To emphasize this the methods suggested in this document encourages objective analysis and planning in partnership with your employer'.[4] This formal framework was issued to all the Association's members and has been used by some employers to back up their own staff development schemes.[5]

Employers can help to encourage employees in their pursuit of personal development by informing them of the possibilities of linking training to qualifications offered by recognized assessment bodies. The role of professional organizations and recognized training bodies for particular library sectors is also important in providing support and innovative training programmes.

Although in-house IT training programmes can be seen in the context of a continuous development strategy for individual learning, they are unlikely to be sufficiently comprehensive in their coverage. They can, however, help individuals decide whether they want to pursue particular topics further.

One possibility which should be encouraged is trainees themselves contributing to the IT training programme. Playing an active part in the educational process can encourage a positive approach by the trainee. Identifying those individuals who would benefit from contributing should not only help with the training programme itself, but also give encouragement to others. Such staff may, for instance, be brought into the programme as trainers, or at least as identifiable opinion leaders whose enthusiasm can be tapped.

2.7 Summary

The smallest change in an organization can bring upheaval and rumours of worrying developments, which may be seen as threatening to individual staff. IT brings with it not merely minor changes; it promises to turn the world upside-down. Staff morale must, however, be maintained and managements must be seen to understand the consequent hopes and threats IT brings and make provision accordingly.

Investment in IT training has an important role here, for it should be designed not only for the imparting of knowledge of particular systems but also to encourage individuals in developing their own interest in the subject. The aim should be to make IT skills an essential element in the CPD of each member of staff.

IT training, therefore, can be said to be important for three main reasons:

- general skills – offering generic computer skills
- particular skills – for specific operations
- navigation skills – enabling individuals to explore IT for themselves.

References

1 Hobson, John, 'The silent revolution at work', *Library Association record*, **98** (4), April 1996, 202–3.

2 Stott, Helen, 'A quick guide to achieving information and library services NVQs', *Managing information*, **3** (3), March 1996, 36–8.

3 Morgan, Steven, 'A personal view of personal development', *Managing information*, **3** (9), September 1996, 41–3.

4 Library Association, *The framework for continuing professional development: your personal profile*, London, Library Association, 1992.

5 Redfern, Margaret, 'Is CPD a growing force?', *Library Association record*, **98** (5), May 1996, 254–5.

3 Training levels

The aim of this chapter is to discuss the different levels of IT training that can exist in library and information services. Training requirements will be similar, even though the types of library may differ. The levels of IT provision will be different across the sectors but will also differ between libraries in the same sector. Staff structures and profiles will also vary and have a bearing, but with work patterns changing almost as rapidly as the technology, prescriptive advice is not possible.

3.1 Training to meet changing needs

As has been referred to earlier, the changes that are taking place across libraries and information services are tranforming traditional staff structures. New skills and changed emphases are breaking down the rigid definitions between professional and non-professional and between one specialty and another.

In some areas the changes are already profound but whether at one extreme or the other, and most of the profession lies somewhere in the middle, the need for IT skills is apparent. However, no course in librarianship can equip an individual for the diverse skills now needed by information professionals. These can be gained only through continuous IT training in the workplace.

As Margaret Redfern points out:

> Some organizations have recognised that the real investment in people is the maintenance of a learning climate which produces and supports a committed skilled workforce. Whether employing long- or short- term contractual staff, paying fees or performance-related pay, the aim is the same, to ensure a capability for continuing high-quality performance in a turbulent environment.[1]

The task of learning IT skills is continuous and complex and, as a result, many organizations fail to cope adequately with the task. The effort needed by the individual in keeping up with the changes can also prove stressful, not only to technophobes. The steep learning curve required in a pressured environment can prove a problem for all but the most determined employee.

All these elements influence the way in which training needs to be organized. Additional factors also have a bearing on what is offered and how it is presented. The organization of training can be based on a matrix in which the level of staff in the hierarchy is overlaid with the level of training that needs to be provided. In addition, this can be matched to the level of funding available for training. Building a matrix in this way, matching the needs and levels of the staff with the training costs, can form the basis of a comprehensible and consistent training programme.

3.2 Type of library

3.2.1 *Academic*

Academic libraries have been at the forefront of the networking revolution that has transformed higher education over the past ten years. The organization of these libraries in particular has had to change in order to respond to the convergence of computing and librarianship. The changing approach to information management is reflected in campus-wide networks, mass access to national and international information resources, the creation of in-house databanks, and the growth of virtual libraries. End-user access to services is making IT training for staff even more necessary, for as user needs become more sophisticated, so the demands on library staff become more complex.

Library staff are caught up with these changes, having to alter their work practices and develop additional skills, increasingly joining with computer staff in mixed teams to provide new services. Change is so rapid that the need for training and re-training is always there, but adequate provision is not often made.

3.2.2 *Public*

Public libraries have not undergone such frantic technological development so far, but change is gathering momentum. In the US, for example, the public library sector is providing public access to the Internet on a wider front each year.[2, 3] Unlike the academic sector, however, network access is less available and Internet connections are often on a dial-up basis. In coming to the problems and possibilities of IT later than their academic colleagues, public librarians should have the opportunity to learn from past experience.

3.2.3 *Special*

Special library development is very dependent on the type of organization involved. Major commercial companies vary considerably both in the importance they give to internal technological change and in their attitude towards their library and information services. The libraries of learned societies, professional associations, local law firms, and charitable organizations generally find themselves without the comprehensive and consistent investment necessary for making well-planned advances in IT.

Whatever the type of library, it is certain that the momentum in each sector will quicken so that all will eventually find traditional library methods, information provision and organization transformed by the end-user revolution. Equally, all will need to train staff to use the technology that is placed before them.

3.3 Type of organizational structure

3.3.1 *Single-site*

The provision of IT training will be affected by the physical organization of the library. For single-site libraries training will, in general, be simpler to organize whatever the type of library. Library size will also have implications for the way training can be organized because of both the numbers of staff involved and the likely availability of adequate facilities for meeting staff training needs.

3.3.2 *Multi-site*

Multi-site libraries are more problematic, with the distance between component parts being an important factor. A wide dispersal of sites will add to the costs of network provision and database licensing, while also adding to the logistic problems of organizing training sessions.

3.3.3 *Urban and rural locations*

The ease with which libraries can organize staff training will also depend on other factors such as geographical location. Urban communications provide easier staff movement while also being more likely to have cable connections to improve electronic communications.

3.4 Type of management structure

The type of management structure of an organization or library can also have an effect on the way staff development is viewed, and this can have a bearing on the way in which IT training is organized. A top-down approach to managing an organization will often see all training in narrow terms, sometimes restricting the possibility of a wider perspective. In such circumstances the training is limited to a person's narrow field of immediate responsibility. In the IT environment this is less likely to prove a successful management approach, for traditional work patterns are becoming harder to maintain. The ability to diversify, adapt and change is an increasingly valuable asset in any workforce.

The team approach to management is much more likely to be successful in responding to change. It is a more worrying approach for insecure managers but should offer individuals far better prospects for personal development in a supportive group environment. In a team environment 'clients often receive a better service produced by the combined knowledge and skills of the whole team'.[4]

3.5 Type of staff structure

The extent of IT training needs will in part be determined by the staff structure of an organization. In libraries, until relatively recently, these structures had changed very little over a long time. It was possible to define professional and non-professional jobs; the convergence of library, computing and other services is changing the old distinctions. Economic factors also have had a bearing on the changing job specifications of staff across the various sectors.

Factors that affect IT training in this context include:

- *Average age.* This may well affect the average level of IT awareness. The implication here is that younger staff will not only have more basic computing skills but will also learn more quickly.
- *Average length of service.* A sound training culture should ensure that regular training programmes are updating staff and maintaining their optimum performance. This cumulative effect should mean that a relatively static staff profile will require a different IT training pro-

gramme to one having to high staff turnover. A lack of IT training over a long period could, however, result in an initial difficulty in motivating staff who may see little reason to change.

- *Types of employment contact.* Not only is the skill base and its development an element in the IT training programme, there is the problem of different employment contracts. Economic factors have been responsible for a growing number of part-time and short-term contract staff. Job sharing is a relatively recent phenomena while other forms of contact such as covering for maternity leave make training programmes even more difficult to organize.
- *Management levels.* The IT needs of library management may be different from the rest of the library staff, there may be a need to develop skills in particular financial packages for example. It may well be true, however, that the IT skills of management will not be as developed as the average staff member. In such circumstances it could be necessary to set up an additional training programme, specially tailored to an individual's needs.
- *Professional librarians.* The closer working relationship between different professional skills in library and information services brings the need for librarians to have a better understanding of IT. An increasing number of librarians are managing mixed teams of librarians and computer officers. IT training in networking technology, e-mail systems and server maintenance may well be needed and should be considered in the creation of a programme.
- *Computer professionals.* As librarians may need training in IT skills to help manage computer professionals, so computer officers may need some IT skills training as well. The training would, of course, be different. Many computer officers need help in adapting their approach to the technology, seeing user interfaces from a user viewpoint. The concerns of librarians about the quality and accessibility of information may also need to be better understood by computer professionals.
- *Support staff.* The development of support staff is also important and the needs of library and computer assistants in a converged service, for example, would reflect that of their professional colleagues in some circumstances.

3.6 Levels of IT skills

To add to all these aspects there is the need to identify the level at which training should be given. Little is to be gained from providing training to those whose skills are already well developed in that area. Compulsory training is counter-productive and wasteful of resources. Equally, there is little point in offering extensive training on computer packages for which adequate built-in tutorials already exist, though adequate information on where such help can be found may well need to be given.

Levels of skills need to be assessed so that appropriate training can be arranged and offered at a suitable time and place for the staff concerned.

It is also helpful to have a comprehensive record of the training history of each employee. This may be kept by the person concerned as a personal development plan, or as an audit of training recorded by the organization itself.

3.6.1 *Basic level*

The need for basic computing skills for individuals has to be met by an organization if an efficient workforce is to be created. These skills can cover the following:

- keyboard skills
- using the mouse
- file management
- disk management
- basic DOS training (where appropriate)
- basic word processing
- e-mail training.

3.6.2 *Intermediate level*

Once a person has mastered the basics of computer management and learned the essential vocabulary of the technology it becomes easier to progress the educational process. The continuation can often be done through the use of the tutorials offered with most good packages.

3.6.3 *Advanced level*

At this level the specialist needs of the individual may need to be catered for by external training. An individual's requirements and development needs will need to be monitored through appraisals and regular contact with the line manager or staff development officer.

3.7 Levels of technology

A positive approach to IT training can exist in a less well-developed IT environment and be very effective in terms of staff satisfaction and development. The converse can also be true: there is no evidence that better equipped establishments provide more coherent training. A successful IT training programme is usually, therefore, the result of the training culture of an organization and not necessarily related to levels of IT development.

3.7.1 *Basic technological provision*

Training in such a situation will inevitably be more problematic, but IT awareness can be raised cheaply through the use of video training packages, demonstrations and lists of recommended reading. In addition, staff can be encouraged to attend external training courses and conferences in order to prepare themselves for future in-house developments.

3.8 Summary

No matter what type of library or organization, the extent of the IT training programme that needs to be put into place is always a fraught question. Should it include all staff or merely those who have an obvious need? What level of training is necessary for each of the groups of staff? These questions can be answered only by individual organizations, for needs and resources have to be balanced.

What this chapter has highlighted is that these divisions should be recognized and thought through. IT training is needed by all members of staff because IT affects them all; it is the definition of their training needs that will place them in a particular category. The need of modern organizations is for a skilled and flexible staff. In this environment IT awareness and competence is important, for it helps ensure that the greatest flexibility is available.

References

1 Redfern, Margaret, 'Is CPD a growing force?', *Library Association record,* **98** (5), May 1996, 254–5.

2 Saunders-McMaster, Laverna, 'Exploring the concept of the virtual library', *Computers in libraries,* September 1996, 49.

3 Stearns, Susan, 'The Internet-enabled virtual public library', *Computers in libraries,* September 1996, 54–7.

4 Tuffield, Joanne, Edgerley, Michelle and Buchanan, Natalie, 'Developing teamwork for more effective client service', *Managing information,* **3** (9), September 1996, 35–7.

4 Training administration

In this chapter the problems of administering and planning IT training will be covered. This has a considerable bearing on the success or failure of IT training. Ensuring that courses are well organized, with good preparation, results in rewarding and positive experiences for trainees. Measuring expected outcomes against the original objectives and ensuring comprehensive feedback to line managers should be supported by sympathetic counselling and support services for those who need them.

4.1 The organization of training

Ideally the library or information service will be part of an organization with a well-established training culture. If this is so, the long-term development of staff will be taken into consideration at all levels. The way in which training is seen will determine both the investment made by the management and the seriousness with which it is viewed by the workforce.

In the UK, Investors in People is a national quality Standard and award. The award is given to organizations 'for effective investment and commitment to the training and development of all their people'. This Standard 'provides a framework, (not a blueprint) for improving business competitiveness, through a planned approach to setting and communicating business objectives and developing people to meet these objectives'. This aim, quoted from the IIP Web homepage(http://www.itl.net/features/iip/whatisiip.html) is achieved through embedding employee training and development firmly in the workplace.

Many organizations have taken up the challenge set by Investors in People and have achieved the approved standard or are working towards it. Even without adopting this approach formally, many employers see the training of their staff as an important investment. Sadly this is not universally the case, and, for a library service based in an organization which fails to see staff development as a priority, it may be more difficult to set up adequately funded training courses. This can be further compounded by a lack of adequate central training facilities to provide a low cost teaching venue.

Given such limitations it is unlikely that comprehensive and dedicated IT courses will be possible. If there is very little backing for training and development across the organization this will be a difficult problem with which to deal. If, however, IT does feature as part of a broader training and development structure it may be possible to use this as the basis for a fuller programme. In either case it would be advisable to invest in those tools which make the process of training less expensive and to encourage more self study and the use of IT as a teaching tool.

IT training courses can be organized in the following ways:

4.1.1 *As part of an organizational staff development programme*

This can be an effective way of undertaking basic IT training for all staff and illustrates the commitment of an organization to the IT needs of its personnele. The need for a smaller separate library IT programme will probably continue to exist in order to meet the specialist needs of information staff.

4.1.2 *As a cooperative programme with similar institutions or departments*

Without a centralized staff development programme, or even in additon to it, it may be possible to join with others to produce a cooperative programme where mutual interests overlap. If full cooperation over training is not feasible, it may well be possible to join together to produce some support materials which could include IT developments.

4.1.3 *Within existing training programmes*

Many libraries have well-established training programmes which cater for the needs of staff. These can include essential elements such as safety procedures, awareness raising visits to other sites or departments, and talks on the library structure and management.

Many of these programmes are regarded by staff, and sometimes their managers, as optional, or are seen solely as catering for the new entrant to an organization. Such training schemes often do nothing to encourage the involvement of staff at all levels. There is evidence to suggest that training programmes are not necessarily very effective in transferring the skills required, but that their effectiveness improves if management is seen to be supportive of the process.[1]

Training, certainly for IT, must be presented as a vital and vibrant element in the workplace and, given the rapid changes that are taking place, its true value should be emphasized. IT should also, of course, be used to help improve the access staff have to training opportunities.

4.1.4 *As an independent programme*

There is much to be said for setting up IT training courses as separate entities. In this way vitality can be maintained and any in-built prejudice against the regular courses can be avoided.

The advantages of organizing a separate IT training programme include:

- a coherent approach can be made to the training
- a better and more consistent allocation of time can be devoted to IT
- a more specialized approach allows the targeting of particular problem areas and attracts more interested individuals
- targeted staff can expect some real value from their participation
- clearly thought-out objectives help ensure that outcomes are definable
- a coherent body of mutual support may emerge which can help improve staff confidence in IT.

4.2 Identifying the need for IT skills

When major technological change has occurred in the work environment, for example the introduction of an electronic office environment or a major system upgrade, the need for skill enhancement is fairly easy to identify and relatively simple to quantify. It is more difficult to pin-point the skills needed by individuals when change is more subtle.

Managers should always try to identify the changes that are affecting an individual's performance and that may be the cause of stress. The continuous enhancement of existing IT packages or the introduction of new ones can cause problems for individuals. The introduction of new interfaces may also bring difficulties. For example, the change of a computer operating system from a DOS to a Windows environment may create problems for a particular individual, or the use of a new computer package, even after a dedicated training session, may cause problems for an operator who may feel embarrassed to admit that he or she is still not coping.

As indicated earlier, the essential purpose of IT training is to meet the perceived needs of both the employer and employee. Such needs can be expressed by staff to their line managers through a number of channels.

It is, however, sometimes difficult for employees to identify and articulate their IT needs. If employees are uncertain about the whole process of IT how can they put their request into a coherent context? If members of staff have problems working with an aspect of a mechanized issue system they are likely to be able to define the problem. If, however, they wish to know more about the Internet it may be difficult to articulate their request, or if they need, for example, to undertake a new task they may not know which spreadsheet package to use or how to find out if there is one that can help.

In the case of IT operations affecting particular functions, such as accessing a supplier's database for acquisition purposes, training may be restricted to those who need access to it for their job. On the other hand, there are functions that are fundamental to library services and here the problem about awareness levels is more difficult to determine. For example, what level of knowledge or expertise should be given to staff about the Internet? Should training be limited only to those with a 'need to know', or is it fundamental for all staff? If so, what levels of training are necessary for the different levels of staff, or should training be the same for all?

In the process of establishing an IT training policy for staff, a number of questions needs to be addressed. This should be done by devising an IT training policy for the organization. Within this the following policies should be considered:

- how will the policy fit into the broader staff development plan?
- is the policy inclusive or exclusive, i.e. will it include LMS functions or not?
- is the policy holistic or function-based, i.e. what are the limits of a 'need to know' policy?
- what grades of staff are covered by the policy?
- what levels of staff are covered by the policy: certain defined levels or all staff?
- how will the policy deal with the special and unusual needs of staff?

In such a changing and dynamic area where there is a growing number of diverse skills being brought together, it would seem that a training policy should be inclusive rather than exclusive.

The importance of an understanding approach by management cannot be overstated. Some evidence of understanding can be achieved by establishing non-threatening feedback mechanisms. Through these, staff can express their personal fears and expectations. Such mechanisms are not easy to establish and winning the trust of staff requires an honest approach. Adequate support materials (see Chapter 5) to which staff can refer if in difficulty are one option.

Though most organizations regard training as an important investment few have invested sufficiently in the process. For those that have, considerable thought has usually gone into the process of feeding back the views of their staff. Many lay down the procedures to be followed and the training routes available.

4.3 Establishing feedback mechanisms

4.3.1 *Staff appraisal/personal development schemes*

These should be important vehicles for assessing the training needs of individuals. Through this method it is possible to gather information about the difficulties being experienced by staff in using current systems and identifying where improved training would help. Although these devices can be excellent vehicles for assessing the immediate problems of an individual they are helpful only in giving a general impression of the need for IT training. As assessment interviews are usually held on an annual or biennial basis, they are too infrequent to cope with the fast-changing world of IT.

4.3.2 *Coaching*

Coaching is a useful way of assessing, amongst other things, the IT training needs of an individual. It is a technique applied particularly when individuals join an organization and gives personal support by someone who is familiar with the requirements of the job. The coaching may well be done by the direct line manager of the individual. The supervision of staff in this way can monitor training needs, some of which may have been expressed. It is important for the person in the coaching role to make their charge aware of the internal IT training opportunities available, while identifying external courses for those specialist needs for which no in-house equivalent exists.

4.3.3 *Mentoring*

Effective mentoring is also useful in assessing the training needs of individuals. A mentor is usually someone in another part of the same organization, or at least not the direct line manager of the individual concerned. A mentor gives a staff member the opportunity to discuss matters, including training needs, with someone not directly involved with the managing process of the individual concerned.

4.3.4 *Internal meetings*

It is not always easy, or desirable, to have discussions on IT problems in large staff meetings. A regular item on a staff meeting agenda can, however, be useful for reporting new developments and seeking feedback on training needs. In addition, a regular substantive discussion, say an annual review, of IT over the past year with a projection of likely forthcoming developments, may encourage discussion about wider training needs.

4.3.5 *Survey questionnaires*

Seeking to identify individual needs across the whole of the staff is probably best undertaken through surveying their requirements and opinions. An annual survey would help in the planning of an IT programme for the following year. A detailed survey would amount to a skills audit (see below). If the intention is to run manageable courses catering for the general needs of the majority of staff then a simple and straightforward survey is what is required. More detailed needs should be picked up at the appraisal stage or through contact with the line manager or mentor.

4.4 Skills auditing

4.4.1 *For planning purposes*

Clear aims and objectives need to be set out before undertaking a skills audit. The intention should be to create a precise picture, at a particular moment, of the IT skills of the staff. This is inevitably a delicate matter and appropriate consultation with staff representatives may be necessary beforehand. It should be made clear that, in undertaking a skills audit, the intention is not to identify the performance of particular individuals but rather to assess the need for an IT training programme and how it may best be targeted.

Such auditing is best done through the use of survey questionnaires which can be filled in anonymously by members of staff. This can be a difficult procedure, especially where staff may be identifiable, for questionnaires may seek to identify the level or grade of staff. Without guaranteed confidentiality, however, a false picture may emerge and this would be counter-productive.

4.4.2 *For assessing outcomes*

Once the skills audit has been established it is possible to make an assessment of the previous year's training programme. The audit can include questions about the programme in general, for example, seeking feedback on the most effective methods of training. Attitude changes to IT should also be discernible over time.

4.5 Setting targets

Many training programmes are run without any clear idea of the expected outcomes. In creating an IT training programme the aims and objectives need to be clear, but so do the expected outcomes. For example:

- *For the individual.* What can a trainee expect from a session and from the programme as a whole?
- *From a particular package or database.* What proficiency can be expected in what areas after the training session? In what new applications should he or she be newly proficient?
- *From an awareness-raising session.* What are the targets for the level of

awareness to be achieved: expert, novice, etc? How well does it fit in with the levels of awareness in related fields?

- *For the trainer.* What are the levels of satisfaction which can be expected from the trainer and made evident in the reporting mechanism? What level of satisfaction can be expected by the trainer especially in relation to the satisfactory performance of any equipment used?

4.5.1 *Limitations of targets*

Targets will be influenced by the training limitations. For example, the capacity of the equipment for effective hands-on training, the reliability of the communications structure for networked training, etc.

4.5.2 *Extending targets*

Planned targets need to consider options for continuing self-directed training if that is appropriate. The level of competence expected at the end of a course and the practice of new skills which participants would have been expected to master can identify further training opportunities. These could form the basis of support documentation for self-training. Trainees could, therefore, not only receive support material to use as an *aide-mémoire* but also be given some guidance for extending their expertise if they wish to do so.

4.6 Measuring outcomes

Measuring outcomes should follow more easily if effective targets have been set. If this has not been done it will depend on the type and level of the course. Measuring outcomes is particularly useful if it is intended that such courses are to be run regularly, for strengths can be identified and built upon. Among the tools that may prove helpful are:

4.6.1 *Assessment forms*

Each training session should end with feedback from the group on the effectiveness of the presentation and value of the training for their particular needs. Many assessment forms are vague and give only a general impression of what resulted, but it is possible to identify whether particular sessions are meeting training needs by linking feedback to target setting.

4.6.2 *Training evaluation*

Immediate feedback at the close of a session may give a misleading reaction. This applies to both good and bad responses, for it is sometimes possible for participants to underestimate the value of a training session only to realize its importance some time later. A more effective test is to make a second survey of participants at a later stage to see how their work, or attitude, has changed since the training.

4.6.3 *Mixed ability groupings*

One of the problems with organizing IT training, especially in small organizations is the difficulty of creating a group profile that benefits equally the learning needs of all the participants. It is often the case that, for logistical or technical reasons, groups of trainees of very mixed ability or different levels of understanding are brought together. This inevitably skews the measurement of learning outcomes, probably causing some dissatisfaction from both those who found a standard too high and those who found it too low.

Awareness of this problem may make it possible to modify the targets for the session, adjusting the learning outcomes accordingly and recording the learning profile as a qualifying comment on the feedback questionnaires.

It may be necessary in such circumstances to provide more trainers and divide the session into groups with similar training needs. Any handouts and exercises should also be geared at the different levels so that, in effect, there are multiple training sessions taking place in one class.

4.7 Feedback into subsequent sessions

The feedback process must be a positive one, and trainees should be reassured that their contribution will be taken into account. Responses should be accepted as a good way of improving the quality of future training.

Changing the teaching approach and method if responses are poor should be done when appropriate. The short- and long-term assessment of teaching will help to give a more honest view of the process, but changing programmes radically if necessary should be taken as a sign of strength rather than weakness.

4.8 Summary

Administering training is more than the devising of programmes and ensuring the presentation of the teaching materials. Training that is truly worthwhile and cost effective should be an essential aspect of the whole staff development process. In this context its administration will seek to identify individual needs, meet them as far as possible, encompass the feedback process and monitor the outcomes.

This chapter has emphasized the advantages of running a separate IT training programme with its own well-defined targets and evaluative structures. In practice, IT is treated as part of the whole staff development process. Sometimes it is a very small part of the whole training picture and, as has been indicated, suffers as a result.

Examples of dedicated IT training programmes are, in fact, difficult to find. The training of IT trainers, through the EduLib (the national network of electronic library accredited trainers) in the UK programme for example, may help to change this. Meanwhile, those existing staff training programmes that contain sessions on IT awareness should be better constructed and include effective feedback and evaluation procedures to help ensure a proper cost benefit to take account of the special demands IT can impose on the workforce.

Reference

1 Burgin, Robert and Smith, Duncan, 'Transfer of training in libraries', *Journal of library administration*, **22** (1), 1995, 51–66.

5 Organizing formal training sessions

This chapter is intended to cover the practical aspects of organizing formal IT training sessions, from planning and budgeting to technical considerations; training through the use of IT is more fully dealt with in Chapter 7. It is impossible to list all the requirements for the various types of training sessions that can be run, but it will endeavour to run through some of the options available for those organizing IT training.

5.1 General preparation

5.1.1 *Seeking consensus*

The need for a true staff development approach has been emphasized elsewhere in this publication. Certainly there ought to be a sense of commitment to training at all levels and this should pervade the whole organization. However, taking front-line staff away from their workplace can cause problems on a number of levels. The training programme must, therefore, be seen, from a management viewpoint, to have a positive impact on performance. From a staff point of view the programme needs to have the support of management and to be of value in itself.

5.1.2 *The training timetable*

Choosing the best time for IT training will depend on the type of library and on other parts of the wider training schedule. For academic libraries, certain times of the year, e.g. the start of a new academic session, are a near impossibility for comprehensive training programmes. However, quieter times during the summer months may find many staff on holiday.

Particular difficulties arise with part-time members of staff in all types of organizations. As they are often employed to help at busy periods, it is always difficult to find a convenient time for their training to take place. For such reasons it may be necessary for training budgets to include provision for additional payments in order that staff can be brought in at convenient times outside, and in addition to, their normal working hours.

5.2 Budgeting for IT training

It must be accepted from the outset that a real commitment to training is not cheap and it is often difficult, in today's economic climate, to provide an adequate budget for training needs. External course costs and their associated travel and subsistence allowances eat into large parts of the training budget. What must be certain is that the training offers value for money, and that may mean a balance between in-house provision and external courses. In-house training should not, however, be offered simply because it is seen as cheaper. Training has to be measurably cost effective and large numbers of staff attending regular sessions can, ultimately, be more expensive than targeting attendance for particular staff at specialist conferences.

When drawing up an IT training programme its full costs will be difficult to estimate, but it is essential to reach some assessment. IT training will require budgetary support and the implications for this must be seriously considered at the start of each financial year. A true assessment of feedback from trainees and the skills audit should influence the way in which the budget is allocated for the subsequent year.

Designated IT training personnel working closely with the Training Officer should be given the task of undertaking devising, administering and monitoring the IT training programme.

5.3 Charges for IT training

5.3.1 *Venue*

If there is not an in-house training facility it may be necessary to hire one. In such an event other charges may also be incurred and clarification needs to be obtained of what exactly the initial hiring charge covers.

5.3.2 *Equipment*

The equipment needed for IT training will almost certainly include: OHP (overhead projector), LCD (liquid crystal display) panel or video projector, computers, software, network connector, telephone line and modem or other form of network connection. For hands-on training sessions additional equipment will be needed and the provision of adequate software configurations (such as Net-Op) providing tutor/student interaction may also be necessary. For external venues hire charges need to be investigated and the provision of adequate technical back-up needs to be clarified.

5.3.3 *Connection charges*

- *telephone charges:* the use of a telephone will involve both line rental and database or other connection charges. When hiring an outside venue it will be necessary to check what these surcharges are likely to be.
- *Internet connection:* an Internet provider will facilitate the interface between the telephone line and Internet protocols. Connection to the Internet may have cost implications. It may be necessary to use an Internet provider who will charge for the use of services.
- *online database hosts:* if the training sessions include connection to charged database services it will be necessary to have a user ID and password for access. Charges will be made for connection time and for searching the database, but both of these can often be reduced for the purpose of training. It is advisable to seek further information from the database host.
- *networked database charges:* if the intention is to give training access to databases such as networked CD-ROMs, it may be necessary to check the existing user licence to ensure that multiple training access is allowable. The response of companies to such a request differs, but most enlightened firms allow such access on a limited basis without extra charge. It is important, however, to seek clearance in all cases if the licence doesn't specifically cover such eventualities.

5.3.4 *Staff charges*

- *instructors:* it may be necessary to employ outside experts as trainers for some sessions and appropriate fees need to be set aside in such instances. However, it is often possible to get commercial database companies to provide a trainer at no cost to the library. Such training sessions are usually offered with free access to the company's databases.
- *technical assistance:* to ensure that training sessions run with the minimum of technical problems, some technical help and advice is recommended. This is more of a problem if there is no technical support in-house. An IT training programme should be supported by an appropriately experienced back-up team. If this is not available it may be possible, in external locations, to enrol the help of the technical team provided by the venue operator, though this will usually be at a cost to the hirer.

5.3.5 *Other costs*

- *breaks:* refreshment breaks may be necessary depending on the length of the training session. It is as well to remember that training is often tiring and better results are achieved with adequate breaks: though less content may be covered the maximum concentration will ensure a better learning outcome.
- *travel:* use of an external venue may well entail travelling costs for staff. These will also need to be included in the total costs of the training sessions.

5.4 Equipment

5.4.1 *Computer terminals*

The running of IT training sessions must presuppose that computers will provide the basic component for the training. Given that this is the case, a cluster of networked computers offers a better opportunity for effective training than standalone machines.

The computers should be as up-to-date as possible for they will offer the versatility necessary for newer applications. Computers in training facilities should be replaced at least every three years, preferably at shorter intervals, to ensure the equipment can meet training needs adequately.

There are a number of networking systems that can be used to link computers to a central master machine, allowing the trainer to control the slave machines centrally. Software options for this process include Net-Op.

5.4.2 *Network connections*

Network connections or a dial-up link are now essential for any IT training. Without them it is impossible to provide Internet training, an essential feature of all IT training today. In higher education network connections are usually available in training rooms but in some other types of library, or in hired training suites, this may not always be the case.

If an external training facility is being used it is essential to know the specification of any network point. If one needs to be installed, advice should be sought from the favoured telephone company in good time. For

Internet demonstrations it will also be necessary to contact an Internet provider who will advise on the configuration you will need on your computer for gaining access to the service. On established networks it is usually necessary to ensure that the workstation being used is registered for the appropriate network domain.

- *Ethernet card:* for communication purposes it is essential to have an appropriate ethernet card loaded in the PC. It may also be necessary to register it for the network domain being used.

5.4.3 *Appropriate software*

It is not possible to identify all the software that will be needed for diverse training sessions but some useful pointers can be given.

Any software package likely to be used on training equipment should be checked for compatibility with the software loaded on the teaching workstations. For example, it is possible to prepare a presentation on one edition of a software package and find that the machine on which it is to be presented has a later incompatible edition.

- **Microsoft Windows**: for most PC applications it is advisable to have Microsoft Windows software loaded so that presentations can be more versatile and therefore more effective.
- **Powerpoint**: using Microsoft Powerpoint can improve a presentation considerably. Ensure, however, that the software is loaded on the training computer that is to be used and that the editions of the software are compatible.
- **CD-ROM software**: load any CD-ROM software as appropriate and test it in good time before it is used in the training session. Networked CD-ROM databases will obviously have to have the training PC linked to the network; demonstrating standalone CD-ROMs may therefore need an additional PC. Be aware that some CD-ROMs take up considerable memory and this should be considered when setting up a training session.

5.4.4 *Displaying the computer image*

There will be a need to offer a projected image from the master terminal, whether the sessions are to be hands-on or not. To project the image from the computer there are several options:

- A fixed video SVGA projector which will usually offer an excellent full colour image. This is the most expensive option.
- A portable video SVGA projector such as an Optima or SharpVision LC projector, which can be linked directly to the master computer. This will provide an excellent image, and is the second most expensive option.
- An LCD panel which will be linked to the computer and placed over a powerful OHP. The quality of these is variable but the more expensive ones provide the best images. LCD panels need a very good OHP projector, preferably with a halogen light source for demonstrations.

5.4.5 *Presenting the information*

The information to be displayed on the screen can be presented in a number of ways:

- OHP transparencies where the information has been downloaded to print from a computer and photocopied on to acetate transparencies can still be an effective means of presentation
- the use of electronic means of presentation, e.g. Microsoft Powerpoint, allows computer presentations to be created and directly projected onto the screen through the LCD or video projector
- the downloading of computer images to slides for projection through a slide projector.

All of these are suitable for displaying information in an organized and professional manner and individual circumstances will dictate which is the best to use. What should be avoided, however, is using transparencies with hand-written presentations. These are often difficult to read and suggest that the training has not been well planned in advance.

Another tip, which applies to any of these options, is to provide only the briefest information on each screen; too much information will either distract the trainees or send then to sleep.

5.4.6 *Using a microphone*

So many trainers fail to use a microphone, even when one is available and convenient. Microphones should always be available and ought to be used. The best demonstrations can be spoiled by trainers failing to project their voices. It is possible that someone in the audience has hearing difficulties and, over the constant hum of the PC and OHP, the strongest voice can be lost.

Clip-on radio microphones are the most effective in a training situation for they allow the trainer to move around the room and still be heard by the audience. It is essential, however, to switch off the device when leaving the training room lest unwanted remarks are broadcast!

5.5 Training location

Many libraries have their own training suite and this should be available as a priority for staff IT training. Without such a facility, establishing a regular programme may be a problem in terms of both organization and budget.

Multi-site libraries may have more than one facility and it is obviously important to choose the most appropriate for the training needs of the group in question. It is also important to ensure that the client group knows which venue is being used and where it is located. Ideally, if there is more than one training suite, it would be advantageous to keep the equipping of them under continuous review and upgrade them on a regular basis. Technical problems with one would then allow the other to be used without too much disruption.

5.6 Preparation

Trainers should be well prepared for the sessions they are going to give.

This should include making sure the training venue is set up and working before the session starts. Rehearsal is also important, in particular checking the timing of the session, the equipment connections and the necessary commands for moving between applications.

Checking should be done an hour or two before each session so that there is time to re-install packages or re-establish connections if necessary. It is an unwritten law that connections will fail when training sessions are under way. This makes adequate preparation even more essential. Well prepared back-up material should be taken into the sessions so that training can continue even if connections have failed.

5.7 Types of training session

It is essential to choose the most appropriate type of training session for the purpose in hand. Options for IT training formats include:

- *Lecture presentation*: this involves a traditional teaching approach with demonstrators using a projected image on a screen (this is probably the least effective method of IT training).
- *Hands-on training*: this allows trainees to undertake training on computer terminals. It can be done in a number of ways, for example with the trainee working through worked examples.
- *Self-teaching sessions*: these give the opportunity for staff to work through computer packages using the in-built tuition options while having a trainer on hand to help out if necessary.
- *Seminar groups*: computer exercises are set and, after a period of time, the group discusses the problems encountered before moving on to the next stage, this is a good method for testing changes or new documentation for training programmes.
- *Self-help workbooks.*

5.8 Distance learning

There is an increasing emphasis on distance learning at most levels of education and, as technology advances and facilities for video conferencing improve, it will become more and more important. A fuller discussion of the possibilities of using IT in the training process is discussed in Chapter 7.

Distance learning offers the following advantages:

- it can save staff time
- it can make a more effective use of scarce resources
- it can save travelling and subsistence costs in multi-site organizations
- the training can be made possible across any distance
- cooperative training with other libraries can be easier to arrange
- presentations can be backed-up with practical exercises using the WWW.

To achieve such results, appropriate technology and adequate investment in training facilities is needed. It also needs good planning, well-trained support staff and excellent trainers. The primary aim of such an investment should always be a better trained staff rather than budgetary savings.

5.9 Support materials

Whether in-house support materials are produced on the Web or in print, time must be set aside for their preparation. There is no doubt that such material enriches the learning experience for those involved but producing them can be time consuming.

Care should be taken when using pre-prepared support documentation as some technical changes may have invalidated the information. This is particularly problematic when providing support material for Web demonstrations; URLs can change at any time.

General guides giving the basic principles of access to systems are often possible to provide without there having to be constant revision, but even here it is best to revise the document at least once a year.

5.10 Feedback

The importance of user feedback has been covered in Chapter 4. The mechanism that should be adopted to obtain an immediate response from trainees does vary. Response forms can either be distributed before the session with any other handouts or handed out during the session. Feedback is important to enable a comprehensive assessment of the training and to assess its value to both the staff member and the organization.

To ensure that response forms are completed it is best to set aside some time at the end of the training session and ask trainees to complete them before leaving. This at least gets a response from all who have attended and ensures a more balanced result.

5.11 Summary

IT training, if it is to be successful, must have a sound technological base. Demonstrating IT applications on equipment which fails, whether because of hardware or software faults does not inspire confidence in the message or the messenger. Every effort should be made to ensure that the technology is in place to offer the advertised programme.

For the non-technical staff who will often be presenting the course it may be essential to have adequate technical back-up. This is so often lacking in traditional library systems and may be one reason why the number of dedicated IT programmes in place is less than is desirable. If the provision of adequate IT training is not being offered because of a lack of technical support, then it throws an interesting light on the depth of the IT provision in libraries. It is additional evidence of the profound need for IT training.

If the future development of IT training programmes depends on investment in equipment and staff, it also demands adequate provision of training facilities. Despite budget constraints, adequate investment in a training facility should be seen as vital. Information professionals need such a facility for their own needs and it is also often possible to recoup some of the investment by hiring out to other organizations.

6 Training session leaders

One of the key elements in the success of any training course is the selection of a good session leader. This chapter is about choosing or training session leaders and then developing their skills in the most productive manner.

6.1 Administration and training

The administration of the training programme and the training itself may well be done by separate personnel. It is important that the person responsible for training is at a senior management level so that training programmes carry some authority.

In most organizations this is usually the case, for the integration of training into the appraisal process makes such senior management input essential. This is also necessary if it is decided to register courses for national awards.

Separating the administration of courses from the trainers is also important, for it releases the training staff for the function for which they are best suited. This ensures that registration, room booking, the organization of response mechanisms, the collation of feedback information and other essential organizational elements are taken away from the trainers. This helps the trainers, who probably have other library responsibilities as well, concentrate on preparation and presentation.

6.2 The training function

The training is often best done by experienced information staff who may well be involved in training the library's clientele. The extent of the training course will obviously determine the number of trainers needed to undertake the training.

In addition, it may be necessary to appoint demonstrators or assistants to help out at certain times. Hands-on sessions, for example, may require more than one person to cope with the questions and problems that inevitably arise. To be effective such sessions need at least one person for every 15 trainees. It may also be necessary to employ assistants to help users at their terminals.

6.3 The role of the trainer

With the use of an IT-based training programme the role of the trainer is different. The need for group interaction may be more limited, but the need for monitoring and advising becomes more difficult and diffuse. In many ways the role of the trainer becomes more active as that of the trainer becomes more passive.

The role of presenter and disseminator of information still exists for the trainer in this novel approach to training, but the skills are used in a different dimension. It is essential that a trainer in this context has the ability to break down the information that needs to be imparted and be able to offer it in a visual way. The trainer has to interact with the programmer in a creative way in order to produce a package that is both technically proficient and accessible to the trainee.

In addition, the trainer can continue to interact with the trainee on a personal level. This would involve establishing the needs of the individual, giving advice on what training programmes will offer, suggesting the best solution to their problems and monitoring the progress being made. It may well be necessary to set trainees deadlines for working through packages and to set tests or seek detailed feedback to ensure proficiency. All this will need to be fed into the process of amending and adapting the packages that are being developed.

6.4 Training the trainers

If the library staff includes an outgoing, charismatic figure with a very good knowledge of IT, then that is the person who should definitely be considered as a good candidate for an IT trainer. However, few libraries are packed with such people and, if there is one, he or she is often doing a valuable job elsewhere in the system.

Good trainers can be trained and there are organizations which can be brought in to run a course on 'training the trainers'. In-house staff development units may well run such courses but it is often the case that they are not fully conversant with the needs of IT trainers. The role of library staff as trainers, for training users or fellow staff, is at last being recognized as an important skill.

In the UK, through the eLib funding project there is now the possibility of library trainers gaining a qualification for their training expertise. This project, called EduLib and based at the University of Hull, is a national programme designed to identify and provide the skills needed by librarians in providing training and to award accreditation to them. The long-term success of such a qualification will depend on the way it will be viewed by employees and employers. That may mean a formal recognition of the qualification through increased monetary rewards. Details of the course are available on the full eLib programme on WWW at http://ukoln.bath.ac.uk/elib/.

6.5 Summary

Many libraries expect their trainers to do much of the administrative work (usually expecting them to do their 'real' job as well). The value of good trainers in the library environment is not as prized as it should be, and yet they are playing an increasingly important role.

The opportunity to offer such individuals a training qualification in the UK is a welcome one and appropriate staff should be encouraged by their managers to undertake the process, while offering rewards for doing so.

Though there will always be a role for trainers, there will also be a growing place for training packages and distance learning. Opportunities for using Web and other packages are already available. These can be made accessible to the staff and fitted into a coherent training programme at little expense to the networked employer.

The development of in-house or cooperative CAL projects for staff IT training has yet to be explored to the full. The opportunity is, however, there for those who have the technology, the technical ability and the ingenuity.

Reference

1 Levy, Philippa, Fowell, Sue, and Worsfold, Emma, 'Networked learner support', *Library Association record*, **98** (1), January 1996, 34–5.

7 Using training packages for IT training

In this chapter the aim is to describe how IT can be used to help provide IT training. Although technology will have to be used in all IT training situations, and a description of the technology needed for traditional presentations is given elsewhere, there are a number of packages which can substitute for these. This chapter describes some of these and how they can be used to form the basis of a training programme.

7.1 Training with IT

Many organizations do not have the facilities required for the provision of training to large numbers of staff. Academic institutions can often provide such facilities and many other large organizations, including companies and local authorities, can do so as well. Even so, the difficulties of organizing staff from every corner of a distributed organization while still ensuring a continuing service can prove difficult. These problems have been outlined in Chapter 5.

Some organizations, even those with reasonable resources, may wish to move away from the traditional approach to training and mobilize IT for the training of their staff. Certainly for smaller and medium-sized organizations this would make very good sense. There are the following advantages in doing so:

- increased flexibility
- reduced costs
- more efficient use of time
- self-paced learning.

Some of the difficulties are:

- the need for a networked environment
- the need to provide an adequate introduction to the technology
- making sure the training is being undertaken by the trainees
- measuring results
- providing supervisory help
- the costs of the software.

Even if this method is chosen for the cost savings that can notionally be made, the provision of this type of training should not be undertaken simply for that reason. There are other costs involved and, though savings will be made in decentralizing the training, other costs will be incurred if real supervision and continuous monitoring is to take place.

7.2 Networked learner support

The importance of networked learner support is developing in a growing number of areas. In some university departments there are computer learning packages in which exercises are automatically marked and assessed, with the results being e-mailed directly to the student's supervisor.

At present, many librarians produce Web guides to their libraries or collections. This energy has been directed for the most part to providing useful guidance to library users. Mutual support for such projects is being developed through an eLib project called *NetLinkS*. The details of which are available on the WWW at http://www.netways.shef.ac.uk/netlinks.htm

There seems little reason why such skills cannot be developed in-house for staff training, so that programmes can be automatically accessed by staff in the workplace. Trainers could share information on a cooperative basis if they so wished. The creation of Web training packages for staff seems an ideal solution for cash-strapped institutions. There seems no reason why these programmes could not be established and sustained. In this way IT training would be comparatively cheap, its effectiveness could be automatically assessed, large training facilities would be needed less, and distance need be no object.

Of course, traditional IT training sessions would still be needed at the outset to give instruction on using the Web successfully.

7.3 Computer based training (CBT)

The concept of CBT has been around in major commercial companies for some time. It is used to increase productivity in many firms by providing interactive learning packages to all workers. Salary levels and progress through the company can depend on the success of a trainee in passing one exercise after another. This form of training is probably not what is wanted for public services where a more holistic approach is usually taken. Here educating the staff is seen as more important than setting levels for individuals to pass through before they can make further progress through the organization.

Even with CBT the need for an experienced trainer is important, for multimedia training does have its limitations. Although, suggests Rex Allen,[1] CBT is excellent for learning basic facts and figures, trainers must ask further questions about the purpose of the training and determine what the organization is expecting from it for both itself and its staff before they consider CBT. He lists the evaluation method created by Donald L. Kirkpatrick. This consists of four levels of questions:

- Level one: did the learners enjoy the training or feel good about it?
- Level two: did the learners remember enough of what they learned to pass the test?
- Level three: are the learners able to demonstrate that they can actually perform what they learned? Has their behaviour changed on the job?
- Level four: is there evidence that the change in the learners created by training has positively affected bottom-line business performance indicators, such as customer retention, repeat business, fewer product rejects or faster turnaround?

The aims and purpose of CBT are evident from these criteria; it is essentially concerned with the maximizing of profit. It is possible, however, to use technology as an aid to IT training without losing the holistic approach so essential to real learning.

7.4 Organizing training with IT

In essence the following problems need to be thought about before devising an IT-based IT training programme:

7.4.1 *The initial training*

For an organization with a low IT threshold which wants to invest in IT training using IT packages, the first problem will be training staff in basic computer skills. It is difficult to see how this can be done without using the traditional approaches covered elsewhere in this book. Packages such as Typing Tutor are helpful in teaching some of the skills needed for computer use, but most novice users need help to overcome the basic fear they have of using a computer.

The proficiency of individual members of staff therefore needs to be gauged at the outset to judge what initial investment is needed to bring everyone up to a standard which allows them to progress on their own.

7.4.2 *The provision of written guidance*

Considerable effort needs to go into the devising of adequate documentation to guide staff to the training packages that are available. Step-by-step guidance should be accompanied by adequate descriptions of the packages and the benefits they will offer the trainee.

Communication should be encouraged so that criticism and innovation can be fed back to the trainer.

7.4.3 *The provision of CAL packages on disc*

There are a growing number of companies producing software training packages for computer assisted learning. These enable trainees to interact with the package and learn at their own pace. The number of subjects covered is considerable. It is possible, for example, to find training packages on:

- operating systems, e.g. DOS 5, Windows 95
- spreadsheet packages, e.g. Lotus 1-2-3, Quattro
- electronic mail, e.g. Microsoft Mail, Lotus cc
- word-processing packages, e.g. Word 6, WordPerfect 5.1
- databases, e.g. dBase IV, Paradox 3.5
- graphics packages, e.g. Harvard Graphics
- personal organizers, e.g. Lotus Organiser.

These can be loaded on standalone workstations or be networked. With the latter, staff can have access at their own workstations and log on to the appropriate packages when it is convenient for them to do so.

7.4.4 *Tutorials*

It should be remembered also that many packages offer a built-in tutorial. These vary in quality but the best of them can be used as a basic introduction to the program. There is little point in creating a teaching package when an adequate tutorial is available. Some staff may need help in working through them at first but training literature can be created to lead individuals to that point if necessary.

7.4.5 *Creating in-house packages*

The technology is available to create in-house training packages, either using expertise in the organization itself or commissioning material from a freelance programmer. A mutual understanding of what is required in terms of standard of material, level of approach and length of exercise can create a tailor-made package that ensures staff have precise training in particular areas. Exercises can be created which automatically download the results to the training supervisor so that the trainee's progress can be monitored. Such packages can be created as a networked CAL package.

7.4.6 *Networked CAL packages*

These can be Windows-based interactive packages covering any aspect of the training programme, or perhaps can give feedback on the training programme as a whole. Software such as Asymetrix Toolbook are ideal for creating attractive presentations which invite interaction by the trainees.

7.4.7 *Devising CAL packages*

Trainers will be needed for running courses but their skills can also be used in other ways. To facilitate distance learning or create packages which can be used to augment the traditional teaching process, trainers can also be encouraged to offer Web pages for staff to access.

The possibilities of adding a Web interface to the training process creates cost-effective and dedicated training facilities for all staff. Using Web technology to devise CAL packages for backing-up the training process can also be an important aspect of training the trainers.

Such packages can become an essential part of the training process and may well offer, in the longer term, the answer to many of the problems that in-house training faces today. With the provision of adequate systems support, Web packages can link to databases and thereby offer testing and assessment facilities. In this way they can play an increasingly vital part in the staff development process.

In devising and developing such training packages trainers will be better equipped for their training role. They will also be developing new skills which could benefit the library organization in other service areas.

7.4.8 *Using CD-ROM training packages*

Once training materials have been created it is possible to download the information on to a CD-ROM. Well designed and indexed packages in this medium have the advantage of being portable and increasingly cheap to produce. It holds out the possibility of creating in-house basic training material and distributing it to all members of the staff as required.

7.5 Using the World Wide Web

7.5.1 *Web-based packages*

Although less sophisticated as interactive packages at present, the use of the Web has the attraction of being easily available across a network. The creation of Web pages is a simple clerical operation and, if well planned, structured information can be fed back through a support database. The creation of such packages through an Intranet can ensure that the package is accessible only to those who need to have access.

7.5.2 *Using Web packages for training*

There are a growing number of Web training packages, usually available free of charge. Some are being developed through various publically supported initiatives; others are provided by the Web browsers themselves.

The interactivity of these programs varies, among the best is the *Tonic* program developed through mailbase@mailbase.ac.uk. This is specifically designed to teach users about the Internet. An example of Web pages supporting IT trainers can be found at the Resources for Trainers Web site at Cornell University (http://www.cit-training.cit.cornell.edu/fortrainers.html).

7.5.3 *Web interfaces to support training*

Even now, by using the World Wide Web, it is possible to link into training modules which have been set up for improving information skills for both users and staff. The Netskills *Tonic* page mentioned above is an excellent example (http://www.netskills.ac.uk/TONIC).

Such distance Internet learning opportunities can be developed in-house in support of locally organized programmes. Cost-effective CAL packages can be set up with the right server support. The creation of Web pages to supply teaching support materials can also be made accessible for training sessions. The major investment here is in the staff necessary to create, monitor and develop such learning packages.

As Marcus Speh has said: 'The Internet as the most comprehensive resource tool ever available, can be the tool and gateway for continuous education and training. In this function, it has something to give to both companies and individuals alike'.[2]

7.6 Creating an Intranet to support training

An Intranet is a Web-based file to which access can be limited to a defined group on a local server. An Intranet offers all the advantages of a Web interface without the worry of having unwanted outsiders view the information pages. It is therefore possible to keep documents on file in a central location and make them accessible to all those who legitimately need to use them. This limited access to a defined group of individuals therefore offers new opportunities for information sharing.[3, 4, 5]

The use of an Intranet for IT training can be limited to offering training packages, in the same way that one may use the Internet. It is also possible to use it as a central location to hold more confidential information for use on a shared basis. For example, the type of information that could be included in this latter category includes commonly held files by trainers, schedules for future training programmes, or support documentation for training sessions.

If an Intranet is set up it will be necessary to ensure that someone has the overall editing responsibility in order for it to function effectively.

7.7 Summary

The IT environment now offers many possibilities for improving the training levels and opportunities for staff in all types of organization. Overcoming the initial fears of computing for those who have little or no experience is still a problem in some areas. Once this has been done, however, probably by the more traditional training process, the way is clear to innovate and experiment in many new ways. What is more, it is possible to monitor and gain automatic assessment of a trainee's performance if that is seen to be important.

References

1 Allen, Rex J., 'The ROI (return on investment) of CBT (computer-based training)', *CD-ROM professional*, **9** (10) October 1996, 34–45.

2 Speh, Marcus, 'Enabling a global community of knowledge', *Aslib proceedings*, **48** (9) September 1996, 199–203.

3 Hannan, Nigel, 'Introducing an Intranet: the management issues', *Managing information*, **3** (10), October 1996, 31–3.

4 Kingston, Paula, 'Project ACORN: using Internet tools to provide local solutions', *Managing information*, **10** (3), October 1996, 42–4.

5 Bevan, Simon and Evans, Janet, 'Managing the library Intranet at Cranfield University', *Managing information*, **3** (10), October 1996, 38–40.

8 Summary

In the next few pages the major points of the publication will be brought together and emphasis will be given to those areas that are essential to the process of IT training. It should enable readers to start the process of setting up training programmes even if it is not possible to invest as much in the process as might be desirable.

8.1 The need for IT training

The rate of technological change is affecting all types of organization and impinging on all their activities. Consequently it is essential to make all staff proficient in those aspects of IT which are necessary to their work. Offering training to staff in just those narrow areas may not, however, be the most effective way of improving performance. It is far more productive in the long term to ensure that staff are comprehensively trained through an appropriate IT training programme.

Among the reasons for this approach are:

- *efficiency gains*: comprehensive IT training for staff is essential if the investment made in hardware and software is to be realized to the full. Internal efficiency gains and improved service potential are achievable only if the staff are confident in the technology and what it can do.
- *greater staff flexibility*: giving staff a thorough understanding of IT will ensure proficiency in basic computer skills resulting in a workforce more able to adapt and change. Rather than being task oriented they will be learning generic transferable skills which will benefit an organization in a fast developing IT environment.
- *improved standards of service*: any organization with a service role has a vested interest in ensuring that the relationship between employees and customers is as positive as possible. The quality of help offered to users will be improved by well-trained staff. In processes involving IT, a thorough understanding of the basic principles of computing, networking and applications software, will ensure a more profound response to any problems presented at an enquiry point or received by telephone.

8.2 Aims and objectives of IT training

The changes that IT can introduce to an organization may be disruptive and disturbing to staff. In an era in which job security is a real worry, anything that is seen as threatening to the workforce is unlikely to be welcomed. A positive approach should therefore be taken by management to provide reassurance and support. One way of doing this is to establish a comprehensive, properly established training programme. This should help:

- *improve staff morale*: explaining the purpose of IT developments and making adequate plans to deal with their consequences is an important management task. In helping staff come to terms with the impact of IT a positive attitude to staff training and development can help maintain staff morale.
- *achieve a sense of communal support*: ensuring that everyone is involved in the training process can help build a sense of communal achievement amongst the participants. Creating a supportive learning environment can bring a mutual regard for individual strengths within the workplace.
- *encourage personal staff development*: the importance of acquiring transferable skills for the staff concerned should help ensure their commitment to the training process. From such an approach should come benefits for the organization in terms of a positive attitude to change, innovatory work practices and greater job satisfaction.
- *offer skills training on particular processes*: although a broad approach to IT training should be taken in order to provide a good contextual basis for the participants, in-depth training in particular skills will need to be offered to specialized personnel. The aims of such training will be to ensure true proficiency by providing adequate support materials and the opportunity for continuous feedback.

8.3 Training levels

Management decisions on training levels for the various categories of staff in an organization are often contentious. Training is sometimes seen as an expensive and superfluous item of expenditure. This publication has attempted to illustrate the important part an IT training programme can play in the performance of an organization.

Guidelines need to be set to help define the levels of training to be provided, to whom, and for what reason. A matrix can be drawn up indicating which levels of staff are to receive which training to what standard.

A training matrix may well be devised on the basis of the inter-relationship of the following elements:

- Grade of staff
- Staff function
- Employment contract
- Need to know
- Levels of training
- Range of training options
- Extent of training
- Levels of ability.

The IT training matrix may well fit in with the levels of training decided upon for other staff training programmes.

What has been emphasized is the need to enlighten all staff in terms of basic IT skills, regardless of their status, because IT is, or is becoming, all pervading. IT awareness is important for an individual's confidence, career prospects, and workplace performance. This must be matched against other aspects such as length of work experience, age profile, staff mobility etc.

8.4 Training administration

Training should be seen as part of the staff development process and the investment made in it will usually reflect an organization's commitment to the process. However, even in those organizations with a high training profile, many do not yet give IT training the importance it warrants.

Staff development programmes should be holistic in approach, enriching an individual and benefiting the organization in equal measure. IT training that is truly worthwhile and cost-effective should be an essential aspect of the whole staff development process.

In meeting individual needs and considering the learning process, training programmes should encompass the process of feeding back the results of training sessions while at the same time establishing a monitoring process.

This process can be made more effective by establishing an independent IT training programme, but few organizations seem to have done so. IT training is often a part of wider staff training programmes, but frequently only a very small part.

The commissioning of an outside consultant to provide the IT training programme may well be the quickest and most effective way of raising the levels of IT awareness in an organization. This is especially so if there is a lack of in-house IT experience. After consultation with staff and the creation of a detailed brief about the needs of the organization, it is often possible for an outside consultant to meet many of the criteria for an effective IT training programme.

8.5 Training sessions

The successful organization of IT training sessions inevitably relies on dependable technology. The provision of an adequately equipped training facility is a desirable feature for the support of IT training programmes. Many organizations cannot offer such provision and may consequently need to hire facilities. This can be an expensive option and may frighten all but the most determined employers.

The use of networked training options, through the Internet or CAL packages, for example, is one developing way in which IT training can be offered. This, of course, begs the question about learning about Internet access in the first place, but suggests a cost-effective structure for those organizations without adequate training facilities or in-house expertise.

If an organization has adequate computing facilities but a limited training budget, it could seek to provide a more diversified training scenario. After offering basic computer skills for those who need them, it could use self-learning Web training programmes or other CAL packages to supplement them.

Such CAL packages can be specially commissioned and could provide a relatively cheap approach to the provision of IT training. It would also ensure that the process of learning encourages greater proficiency in the use of computing. What is essential is that the elements of the package, be they through distance learning or by formal sessions, should form the basis of a personal development package for each individual. These are being monitored and enhanced over time.

8.6 Who conducts the training?

Participation in any training programme should be a positive experience and ensuring this requires considerable investment in time and planning as well as individuals with good training skills. Trainers are also often expected to do much of the administrative work of which there can be a great deal if proper support materials and feedback are to be provided.

The EduLib project in the UK is offering IT trainers in the information professions a training qualification. This is an important move and staff should be encouraged by their managers to undertake the process.

8.7 Conclusion

The purpose of this publication has been to help open up the debate about IT training in library and information services. The IT needs of staff in any organization are continuous and growing and have to be addressed if it is to run efficiently and effectively. They are even more essential for a profession whose whole purpose and function is concerned with the provision, delivery and dissemination of information.

These needs can be catered for through a dedicated in-house training programme, a hybrid programme with IT as part of a larger staff development programme, a distance learning option using bought-in, ready-made packages or a mixture of all of these.

Whatever is decided as the best option for IT training, it is undoubtedly an essential element in the management of any organization as the Millennium approaches.

Bibliography and further reading

Allen, Rex J., 'The ROI (return on investment) of CBT (computer-based training)', *CD-ROM professional*, **9** (10), October 1996, 34–45.

Amitd, C. R., 'Becoming a learning organisation', *Training and development*, March 1993, 13–14.

Bevan, S. and Evans, J., 'Managing the library Intranet at Cranfield University', *Managing information*, **3** (10), October 1996, 38–40.

Biddiscombe, Richard (ed.), *The end-user revolution: CD-ROM, the Internet and the changing role of the information professional*, Library Association Publishing, 1996, 35–42.

Burgin, R.G. and Smith, D., 'Transfer of training in libraries', *Journal of library administration*, **22** (1), 1995, 51–66.

Burgoyne, J., 'Feeding minds to grow the business', *People management*, 21 September 1995, 22–5.

Dewey, B.I., *Library jobs: how to fill them, how to find them*, Phoenix, AZ, Oryx Press, 1987.

Educational development for higher education library staff: a proposal submitted in the training and awareness area of the Funding Councils' library programme, Hull, Edulib, 1996, 11p.

Freeman, M., 'A sense of direction: librarianship and CPD', *Librarian career development*, **2** (3), 1994, 26–8.

Garrett, B., 'An old idea that has come of age', *People management*, 21 September 1995, 25–8.

Garrod, P., 'Skills for the new professional', *Library Association record*, **98** (1), 1996, *Library technology supplement*, 99–100.

Guidelines for training in libraries, London, The Library Association, 1980.

Hannan, N., 'Introducing an Intranet: the management issues', *Managing information*, **3** (10), October 1996, 31–3.

Hefner, D., 'The CBT (r)evolution and the authoring engines that drive it', *CD-ROM professional*, **9** (10), 1996, 46–65.

Higher education librarians as educators: a training needs analysis, Hull, Edulib, 1996(?), 15p.

Hobson, J., 'The silent revolution at work', *Library Association record*, **98** (4), 1996, 202–3.

Hyams, Elspeth, 'Professional futures – why the prospects are so rosy', *Aslib proceedings*, **48** (9), 1996, 204–8.

Investor in people, your handbook, Dudley Training and Enterprise Council (TEC), 1995(?), 45p.

Jones, P., 'The mystery of the IT managers', *Infomatics*, **14** (9) September 1993, 34–40.

Kingston, P., 'Project ACORN: using Internet tools to provide local solutions', *Managing information*, **10** (3), October 1996, 42–4.

Lacey Bryant, Sue, *Personal professional development and the solo librarian*, London, Library Association Publishing, 1995. (Library Training Guides series).

Levy, P., Fowell, S. and Worsfold, E., 'Networked learner support', *Library*

Association record, **98** (1), January 1996, 34–5.
Levy, P., Fowell, S. and Worsfold, E., 'Networked learner support', *Library Association record*, **98** (1), January 1996, 34–5.
Library Association, *The framework for continuing professional development: your personal profile*, London, Library Association, 1992.
Morgan, S., 'A personal view of personal development', *Managing information*, **3** (9), September 1996, 41–3.
Morris, B., *Training and development for women*, London, Library Association Publishing, 1993. (Library Training Guides series).
Mumford, A., 'How managers can become developers', *Personnel management*, June 1993, 42–5.
'The NVQ framework', *NVQ monitor*, Winter 1995, 16–18.
Pickles, N. and Totterdell, A., 'Towards a better workforce', *Library Association record*, **98** (2), February 1996, 91–3.
Redfern, M., 'Is CPD a growing force?', *Library Association record*, **98** (5), May 1996, 254–5.
Saunders-McMaster, L., 'Exploring the concept of the virtual library', *Computers in libraries*, September 1996, 49.
Scarsbrook, P., 'Information and library services: S/NVQs embace IT', *OCLC systems and services*, **12** (1), 1996, 14–20.
Speh, M., 'Enabling a global community of knowledge', *Aslib proceedings*, **48** (9), September 1996, 199–203.
Stearns, Susan, 'The Internet-enabled virtual public library', *Computers in libraries*, September 1996, 54–7.
Stott, H., 'A quick guide to achieving information and library services NVQs', *Managing information*, **3** (3), March 1996, 36–8.
Sweet, P., 'Still crazy after all these years', *Infomatics*, **15** (8), August 1994, 15–18.
Tseng, G., Poulter, A. and Hiom, D., *The library and information professional's guide to the Internet*, London, Library Association Publishing, 1995.
Tuffield, J., Edgerley, M. and Buchanan, N., 'Developing teamwork for more effective client service', *Managing information*, **3** (9), September 1996, 35–7.
Wakeling, W., 'Meeting the demand for CD-ROM databases. Case study 1: academic libraries', in Biddiscombe, R. (ed.), *The end-user revolution: CD-ROM, the Internet and the changing role of the information professional*, London, Library Association Publishing, 1996, 35–42.
Whetherly, J., *Management of training and staff development*, London, Library Association Publishing, 1994. (Library Training Guides series).
Winship, I. and McNab, A., *The student's guide to the Internet*, London, Library Association Publishing, 1996.

Useful addresses

Aslib
The Association for Information Management
20–24 Old Street
London EC1V 9AP
Tel: +44 (0)171 253 4488
Fax: +44 (0)171 430 0514

British Computer Society
1 Sanford Street
Swindon
Wiltshire SN1 1HJ
Tel: +44 (0)1793 417417

EduLib: the national network of Electronic Library accredited trainers
Professor David McNamara, Director,
EduLib Project
University of Hull
Hull HU6 7RX.
e-mail: d.r.macnamara@educ.hull.ac.uk.

IBM Global Campus
http://www.training.ibm.com/ibmedu/

Independent Education Brokers (IEB)
Graphic House
Station Approach
Chipstead
Surrey CR5 3TD
Tel: +44 (0)1737 552669
Fax: +44 (0)1737 553326
e-mail: dbeaney@ieb.co.uk
http://www/ieb.co.uk

IMPEL 1 & 2: Impact on People of Electronic Libraries. Monitoring organizational and cultural change.
Professor Joan Day (Project Co-Leader)
Department of Information & Library Management
University of Northumbria at Newcastle
Newcastle-upon-Tyne NE1 8ST
e-mail: joan.day@unn.ac.uk

Graham Watson (Project Co-Leader)
Faculty Librarian
Health, Social Work & Education,
Information Services Department
University of Northumbria at Newcastle

Newcastle upon Tyne NE1 8ST
e-mail: graham.walton@unn.ac.uk

The I.T.Training Unit
A unit of the business development and training consultancy of Surrey County Council.
Thames House
Portsmouth Road
Esher KT10 9AD
http://www.surreycc.gov.uk/it-training

Institute of IT Training
Institute House
University of Warwick Science Park
Coventry CV4 7EZ
Tel: +44 (0)1203 418128
Fax: +44 (0)1203 690164
e-mail: info@iitt.org.uk
http:www.iitt.org.uk/in-inst.htm

NVQ/SNVQ
Information and Library Services Lead Body
c/o The Library Association
7 Ridgmount Street
London WC1E 7AE
Tel: +44 (0)171 255 2271
Fax: +44 (0)171 637 0126
http://www.ilsnvq.org.uk/ilsnvq/

Joint Information Services Committee (JISC)
Northavon House
Coldharbour Lane
Bristol BS16 1QD
Tel: +44 (0)117 931 7230
Fax +44 (0)117 931 7255

The Library Association
7 Ridgmount Street
London WC1E 7AE
Tel: +44 (0)171 636 7543
Fax: +44 (0)171 636 3627
e-mail: info@la-hq.org.uk

National Computing Centre Ltd
Oxford Road
Manchester M1 7ED
Tel: +44 (0)161 228 6333
Fax: +44 (0)161 237 5330

National Council for Educational Technology
Milburn Hill Road
Science Park
Coventry CV4 7JJ
e-mail: enquiry-desk@ncet.org.uk

Netskills: Network skills for the UK higher education community
University Computing Service,
University of Newcastle
Newcastle upon Tyne NE1 7RU
Tel: +44 (0)191 222 5000
Fax: +44 (0)191 222 5001
e-mail: http://www.netskills.ac.uk/

Universities and Colleges Information Systems Association (UCISA)
Secretary: I.D.Griffiths
Head of Computing Services
Nottingham Trent University
Burton Street
Nottingham NG1 4BU
Tel: +44 (0)115 948 6444
Fax: +44 (0)115 948 4266

Membership Enquiries: UCISA Aministrator
Information Services
University of Central England
Perry Barr
Birmingham B42 2SU
Tel: +44 (0)121 331 6234
Fax: +44 (0)121 331 6789

University & Colleges Staff Development Association (UCoSDA)
Ingram House
65 Wilkinson Street
The University of Sheffield
Sheffield S10 2GJ
Tel: +44 (0)114 282 4211
Fax: +44 (0)114 272 8705
e-mail: ucosda@sheffield.ac.uk

Appendices

1 A training needs analysis questionnaire

2 An IT training course for university staff

3 A university library computing survey questionnaire

Appendix 1 A training needs analysis questionnaire

UNIVERSITY OF BRISTOL LIBRARY

Training Needs Analysis Questionnaire

Name:..Post:...

Please return to.. by: ....

Appendix 1 **continued**

The Staff Development Group have taken on a more proactive role in providing training.

There are two aspects to training, one relates specifically to the job, the other to personal development.

This questionnaire forms part of a process of identifying the training needs of all staff with the aim of enabling you to do your job better, by building on existing skills. (Training for personal development will continue to be available).

Four members of staff will be introducing the Training Needs Analysis to groups of Library staff. There will be eight groups covering all members of staff. The completed questionnaires will be reviewed by the four members of staff. All staff within each group will be invited to attend a short meeting to build on the information provided in the questionnaire and to clarify any areas of uncertainty.

It is intended to feed the results of the training needs analysis into the staff development programme.

The four members of staff who will be introducing the TNA are:

Heather Bailey
Sue Davies
Karen Thomas
Michael Wall

October 1995

Appendix 1 **continued**

These questions are intended to provide some background about the work you do, give you the opportunity to indicate which areas you feel you need to develop and to identify topics for training which are not covered on the next page.

1. **Outline the main tasks you are involved with?**

2. **What skills would you like to develop in order to become more effective in your work?**

3. **Are there areas of training you feel are not covered on the next page?**

Appendix 1 continued

The following topics have previously been identified as useful.

Please indicate which would be of use to you, and add some information about what aspect would be especially relevant to you in your job.

Area of training	Tick if interested	What aspects?
Customer care		
Health and safety		
Team-work skills		
Teaching and learning skills		
Planning induction events		
Understanding how the University works		
Financial training		
Time management		
Report writing		
Identifying user needs		
Management of people		
Interpersonal skills		
IT training		

Appendix 2 An IT training course for university staff

Information Technology Training 7

Section Seven ~ Information Technology (IT) Training Courses

Management Services Group (MSG) provides IT Training Courses for all University staff.

For those who have no experience in the use of the keyboard a keyboard training package is available. Further courses introduce staff to the PC and the network environment of the University and to the EMail package Pegasus Mail, which is available for use by all staff. Generic packages such as WordPerfect and Quattro Pro are offered at various levels of expertise. A Workbased Learning Module in Wordprocessing is available for those interested in obtaining credit points towards a University Certificate.

Courses are also available for users of the Corporate Student System (written and maintained by MSG). Standard courses are outlined below but special courses are set up as the system is developed. Staff are invited to prototype new areas of work with MSG prior to release.

Training is also provided for the use of *CFacs*, the University's finance system.

There is one staff IT training room in the University. It is located at Bounds Green campus on Level 4 (Room 4-13) and is spacious and well equipped, with eight networked 486s and a LaserJet printer. We are happy to provide training on other campuses during semester breaks or at any time when a School or Service can arrange access to a suitable room for training four or more people.

Course material is provided to all attendees and a "Help Line" is available to answer queries after the course has been completed. The "Help Line" telephone number is Ext. 6464.

All of our courses will be advertised as widely as possible throughout the University.

To enquire about available courses or book yourself on to a course, please telephone Management Services Group on Ext. 6442.

Appendix 2 continued

	General	
69	Introduction to Personal Computers & Networks	*1 half day*
69	Introduction to P-Mail (DOS)	*1 half day*
70	Introduction to P-Mail (Windows)	*1 half day*
70	Introduction to Windows 3.1	*1 half day*
	Word Processing	
71	Introduction to WordPerfect 5.1 (DOS)	*2 half days*
71	Intermediate WordPerfect 5.1 (DOS)	*3 half days*
72	Advanced WordPerfect 5.1 (DOS) - Large Documents	*1 half day*
72	Advanced WordPerfect 5.1 (DOS) - Macros & Graphics	*1 half day*
72	Advanced WordPerfect 5.1 (DOS) - Sort & Merge	*1 half day*
73	Introduction to WordPerfect 6 for Windows	*2 half days*
	Extending WordPerfect 6 for Windows Skills:	
73	1 Columns & Tables	*1 half day*
74	2 Sort & Merge	*1 half day*
	Internet	
74	Getting Started on the Internet using the NETSCAPE Browser	*1 half day*
	Spreadsheets	
75	Introduction to Lotus 1-2-3 (Rel. 2.3)	*2 half days*
75	Introduction to Quattro Pro 6 for Windows	*2 half days*
	Corporate Student System	
76	CSS for Administrative Staff	*3 half days*
76	CSS for Admissions Office Staff and Assessment Office Staff	*3 half days*
76	CSS Workshop/Refresher Course	*1 half day*
77	CSS for Academic Staff	*1 half day*
77	CSS Reports	*1 half day*
	CFACs	
78	*CFACs* Purchase Order Entry for Inputters	*2 half days*
78	*CFACs* for Authorisers	*2 half days*

Appendix 2 continued

General

Introduction to Personal Computers & Networks 0.5 day

For all staff who want to gain a general awareness of Personal Computers, MS-DOS and Networks.

The course has been designed to give a basic understanding of the main hardware and software components of computing as well as a general awareness of the network system in operation at Middlesex University. Trainees will learn how to log in to the network from any of the campuses within the University and will understand how to run a variety of applications via the network.

Pre-Requisites: *None.*

Introduction to P-Mail (DOS) 0.5 day

For all staff who wish to use electronic mail for internal or external purposes.

The course has been designed to teach members of staff how to use the DOS version of Pegasus Mail (PMail) to send electronic messages to and receive electronic messages from other members of staff within Middlesex University as well as individuals with electronic mail who might be located anywhere in the world.

course content

- Using the Address Book
- Creating Draft Messages
- Creating Folders & Distribution Lists
- Attaching & Extracting documents

Pre-Requisites: *You should have a basic knowledge of PCs and MS-DOS and must be familiar with the QWERTY keyboard. You should also have a working Novell Network account.*

❖ **PMail courses for AppleMac users can be arranged for groups of four or more on request.**

Appendix 2 continued

Introduction to P-Mail (Windows) 0.5 day

For all staff who wish to use electronic mail for internal or external purposes.

The course has been designed to teach members of staff how to use the Windows version of Pegasus Mail (PMail) to send electronic messages to and receive electronic messages from other members of staff within Middlesex University as well as individuals with electronic mail who might be located anywhere in the world.

course content

- Using the Address Book
- Creating Draft Messages
- Creating Folders & Distribution Lists
- Attaching & Extracting documents

Pre-Requisites: *You should have a basic knowledge of PCs and MS-DOS and must be familiar with the QWERTY keyboard. You should also have a working Novell Network account. You are expected to have either attended the Windows Introductory course or have reached a similar level of knowledge.*

Introduction to Windows 3.1 0.5 day

The course has been designed to give a general awareness of the Windows operating system. By the end of the course you will be able to run a variety of applications via Windows and will have gained a basic understanding of the way in which the system can enable you to switch between applications, copy and move text and graphics between applications, organise directories and files easily and customise your working environment (i.e. position of windows and icons, mouse control, etc.)

Pre-Requisites: *You should have a basic knowledge of PCs and MS-DOS and must be familiar with the QWERTY keyboard. You should also be familiar with the basic Windows skills (including use of the mouse) that are covered in the Windows Tutorial.*

Information Technology Training

Appendix 2 continued

Information Technology Training

Word Processing

Introduction to WordPerfect 5.1 (DOS) 2 x 0.5 day

For all staff who want to learn the basic skills of word processing.

The basic functions of WordPerfect 5.1 will be covered which will enable you to fulfil general office requirements. Features covered include:

course content

- Creating, editing and printing a document
- Document layout (Margins, Justification, Tabs, Indents)
- Using the University standard memo
- Using the Spell Check & Thesaurus

Pre-Requisites: *You should have a basic knowledge of PCs and MS-DOS and must be familiar with the QWERTY keyboard.*

Intermediate WordPerfect 5.1 (DOS) 3 x 0.5 day

This course is aimed at WordPerfect 5.1 users who are familiar with the basic word processing features and wish to use more advanced features of the product. Features covered include:

course content

- Tables
- Outline/Paragraph Numbering
- Columns
- Simple Macros
- Mail Merge
- Simple Sort

Pre-Requisites: *You are expected to have either attended the WP5.1 Introductory Course or have reached a similar level of knowledge.*

Appendix 2 continued

Advanced WordPerfect 5.1 (DOS) 0.5 day

Large Documents

The course is designed for WordPerfect 5.1 users who want to learn how to create and handle large documents. Advanced editing techniques and presentation methods including:

course content

- Headers and Footers
- Footnotes
- Table of Contents
- Master Documents

Pre-Requisites: *You are expected to have either attended the WP5.1 Intermediate course or have reached a similar level of knowledge.*

Advanced WordPerfect 5.1 (DOS) 0.5 day

Macros & Graphics

The Macro feature is a powerful tool with innumerable applications. The course will demonstrate new ways of applying them to the work situation. It will include creating: simple macros, temporary macros, and pause macros.

The Graphics feature lets you incorporate pictures, images, lines and shading into your document. The capability to mix text and graphics in the same document makes it easy to produce newsletters, instructional material and other documents where figures, diagrams etc are needed.

Pre-Requisites: *You are expected to have either attended the WP5.1 Intermediate course or have reached a similar level of knowledge.*

Advanced WordPerfect 5.1 (DOS) 0.5 day

Sort & Merge

The course is aimed at WordPerfect 5.1 users who wish to use it as a simple database for sorting and selecting and also for advanced mail merge.

Pre-Requisites: *You are expected to have either attended the WP5.1 Intermediate course or have reached a similar level of knowledge.*

Appendix 2 continued

Information Technology Training

Introduction to WordPerfect 6 for Windows 2 x 0.5 day

This course has been designed to cover the basic functions of WordPerfect 6 for Windows.

course content

- Creating, editing and printing a document
- Document layout (Margins, Justification, Tabs, Indents)
- Using the University standard memo
- Using the Spell Check

Pre-Requisites: *You should have a basic knowledge of PCs and MS-DOS and must be familiar with the QWERTY keyboard. You are also expected to have either attended the Windows Introductory course or have reached a similar level of knowledge.*

Extending WordPerfect 6 for Windows Skills

1 Columns & Tables 0.5 day

The course has been designed for WordPerfect 6 for Windows users who want to create and modify columns and tables.

course content

- Using the Abbreviations and Quick Correct features
- Finding & Replacing text
- Creating & modifying columns (newspaper & parallel columns)
- Creating & modifying tables

Pre-Requisites: *You are expected to have either attended the WordPerfect 6 for Windows Introductory course or have reached a similar level of knowledge.*

Appendix 2 continued

Information Technology Training

2 Sort & Merge 0.5 day

This course has been designed for users who want to use the Merge and Sort features in WordPerfect 6.1 to produce letters, envelopes, mailing labels, contracts, phone lists, memos or documents.

course content

- Creating Data Files
- Creating Form Files
- Merging Data
- Merging data into Labels and Tables
- Sorting old and new data

Pre-Requisites: *Staff should have previously attended the WordPerfect 6.1 Introductory sessions, or have reached a similar level of competence.*

INTERNET

Getting Started on the Internet using the Netscape Browser 0.5 day

This course has been designed as an introduction to the **World Wide Web** using the browser **Netscape.**

course content

- Locating addresses
- Adding and editing Bookmarks
- Navigating the WWW
- Types of Locations
- Setting Preferences
- Using Search Engines

Pre-Requisites: *Staff are expected to have either attended the Windows Introductory course or be familiar with using windows.*

Appendix 2 continued

Introduction to Lotus 1-2-3 (Rel. 2.3) 2 x 0.5 day

On this course the basic aspects of Lotus 1-2-3 will be covered. At the end of the course you will be able to create spreadsheets of any size inputting both data and formulae. You will also be able to print reports from spreadsheets.

Pre-Requisites: *You should have a basic knowledge of PCs and MS-DOS and must be familiar with the QWERTY keyboard.*

Introduction to Quattro Pro 6 for Windows 2 x 0.5 day

The course has been designed to cover the basic functions of the Windows version of Quattro Pro. At the end of the course you will be able to create spreadsheets of any size inputting both data and formulae. You will also be able to print reports from spreadsheets.

Pre-Requisites: *You should have a basic knowledge of PCs and MS-DOS and must be familiar with the QWERTY keyboard. You are also expected to have either attended the Windows Introductory course or have reached a similar level of knowledge.*

Appendix 2 **continued**

CORPORATE STUDENT SYSTEM

CSS for Administrative Staff 3 x 0.5 day

For administrative staff working in a Student Office, SET/SAP Office or School office who need to access the Corporate Student System for updating information about students and their study programmes.

course content

- Understanding the Common Academic Framework
- Working within the appropriate 'business role' of the CSS
- Understanding how to access the CSS via the University Network
- Using the menu options offered
- Hands on use of 'Forms' to retrieve and when necessary change information held on the database
- Use of 'Reports' to be printed, viewed on screen or saved to a file

Pre-Requisites: *None.*

CSS for Admissions Office Staff and Assessment Office Staff 3 x 0.5 day

Separate courses are arranged for staff working in these areas covering the appropriate business role and ensuring staff are competent to input and change data as the changing demands of the annual schedule demand. The areas include those covered in the above course as well as downloading information to WordPerfect.

CSS Workshop/Refresher Course 0.5 day

For staff who wish to refresh their knowledge of the Corporate Student System.

Special sessions can be arranged for a particular School or Service area on request.

Appendix 2 continued

Information Technology Training

CSS for Academic Staff 0.5 day

For academic staff who wish to access the Corporate Student System to facilitate their administrative and academic advisor needs.

course content

- The Common Academic Framework
- Understanding how to access the CSS via the University Network
- Using the menu options offered
- Hands on use of 'Forms' to retrieve information held on the database
- Use of 'Reports' to be printed, viewed on screen or saved to a file

CSS Reports 0.5 day

For staff who wish to explore the latest reports offered by the Corporate Student System.

course content

- New reports
- Printing reports
- Examining a report on the screen
- Downloading a report to file

Appendix 2 continued

CFACs

CFACs Purchase Order Entry for Inputters 2 x 0.5 day

This course has been designed to include all the information required for users to be able to input an online purchase order, monitor the progress of an order, add new suppliers and new supplier order addresses.

course content

- Purchase Order Entry
- Creating the Header
- Specifying Order Items and Text Lines
- Headers and Footers
- Editing and Deleting Purchase Orders
- Purchase order Enquiries
- Supplier Enquiries
- New Supplier Submissions
- Supplier Order Sites

Pre-Requisites: *Staff should be familiar with the QWERTY Keyboard, and be responsible for raising orders within their department. Staff must attend the training sessions before being allowed access to the live system.*

CFACs Purchase Order Entry for Authorisers 2 x 0.5 day

This course has been designed to include all the information required for users to be able to authorise an online purchase order and control budgets.

course content

- Purchase Order Entry
- Creating the Header
- Specifying Order Items and Text Lines
- Headers and Footers
- Editing and Deleting Purchase Orders
- The Role of the Authoriser
- General Ledger Enquiry
- Trial Balance Report
- Residual Budget Enquiry

Pre-Requisites: *Staff who are responsible for authorising orders must attend the training session before being allowed access to the live system. Staff who have previously attended the Inputters course, but want to run reports, need only attend the second half day course for Authorisers.*

Appendix 3 A university library computing survey questionnaire

Edinburgh University Library
Staff Development
Computing skills minimum requirements

File management/best practice
Concept of drives and directories particularly with regard to the network
Constraints on file naming and extension conventions
Locate files using DOS and Windows
Search for files with particular extensions (using wildcards)
Able to move around directories and drives
Saving files in directories
Creating a personal directory
Able to copy a file onto a floppy disk for transferral or backup
Able to copy a file from floppy disk to PC
VIRUS CHECKING

Windows/Keyboard
Keyboard - tab, control, function keys, PageUp PageDown, number pad etc.
Point and click
Groups
Icons
Open applications
Maximise, minimise, scroll bars, menus, toolbars
Task manager
Control panel
Exit session

Pmail
Read received mail
Search for mail address (internal)
Send mail
Delete mail

Word
Open a file
Create a new file
Close a file
Type a basic unformatted document
Save and retrieve file
Save As
Open a document not created in Word or without .doc extension
Spell checker

Netscape
Concept of hypertext links
Concept and location of home page
Navigation buttons
Navigation history
Locating resource from known URL
Locating resource from file
Tips - switch off images, use in morning etc.

Appendix 3 continued

Edinburgh University Library
Staff Development
Computing skills questionnaire

This questionnaire aims to assess the training needs of all Library staff. If you feel competent in the areas described, tick the adjacent box. Please take some time to think about your skills and answer the questions honestly. If you are unsure of your competence in an area, or do not understand what is described, leave the tick-box blank.

1. File management - can you

a) Identify drives and directories on a local PC or on the network? ❒
b) Name files correctly and use extension conventions? ❒
c) Locate files using DOS and Windows? ❒
d) Search for files with particular extensions (using wildcards)? ❒
e) Move around directories and drives? ❒
f) Save a file in a particular directory? ❒
g) Create a personal directory? ❒
h) Copy a file onto a floppy disk for transferral or backup? ❒
i) Copy a file from floppy disk back to a PC? ❒
j) Use the virus checker? ❒

2. Windows / Keyboard - can you

a) Identify what all the keys on a computer keyboard are for? ❒
b) Point and click using a mouse? ❒
c) Use the program manager in windows? ❒
d) Identify groups and icons in windows? ❒
e) Open a windows application? ❒
f) Maximise and minimise windows, use scroll bars, menus and toolbars? ❒
g) Use the task manager in windows? ❒
h) Use the control panel in windows? ❒
i) Exit from an application and from Windows? ❒

3. Pmail - can you

a) Read received mail? ❒
b) Send mail? ❒
c) Send internal mail to someone whose address you don't know? ❒
d) Delete mail? ❒
e) Create and manage mail folders? ❒

Appendix 3 continued

4. Word for Windows - can you

a) Open a file? ❐
b) Create a new file ❐
c) Type a basic unformatted document? ❐
d) Save a file? ❐
e) Close a file? ❐
f) Use the Save As function? ❐
g) Open a document not created in Word or without a .doc extension? ❐
h) Use the spell checker? ❐

5. Netscape - can you

a) Identify and define what a hypertext link is? ❐
b) Identify and find your institution's home page? ❐
c) Use navigation buttons? ❐
d) Use the navigation history? ❐
e) Locate a resource from a known URL? ❐
f) Locate a resource from a local file? ❐

Thank you for taking the time to answer these questions. They will help greatly in the creation of suitable training programs for library staff.

Index